Reconciliation
AND REPARATION
Preaching Economic Justice

Sister Gloria,

JOSEPH EVANS
Foreword by J. Alfred Smith Sr.

Please read and make us better;

Joseph Evans

JUDSON PRESS
PUBLISHERS SINCE 1824
VALLEY FORGE, PA

Philippians 3:10-11

To Grant and Grace

Judson Press has made every effort to trace the ownership of all quotes. In the event of a question arising from the use of a quote, we regret any error made and will be pleased to make the necessary correction in future printings and editions of this book.

Bible quotations in this volume are from the New American Standard Bible, © 1960, 1962, 1963, 1968, 1971, 1972, 1973, 1975, 1977 by The Lockman Foundation. Used by permission. / HOLY BIBLE, New International Version®, NIV®, copyright © 1973, 1978, 1984, 2011 by Biblica Inc. Used by permission. All rights reserved worldwide. / The New Revised Standard Version of the Bible, copyright © 1989 by the Division of Christian Education of the National Council of the Churches of Christ in the United States of America. Used by permission. All rights reserved.

Interior design by Beth Oberholtzer Design.
Cover design by Wendy Ronga, Hampton Design Group.

Library of Congress Cataloging-in-Publication data

Names: Evans, Joseph (Dean of Morehouse University School of Religion), author.
Title: Reconciliation & reparation : preaching economic justice / Joseph Evans ; foreword by J. Alfred Smith Sr.
Other titles: Reconciliation and reparation
Description: first [edition]. | Valley Forge : Judson Press, 2018.
Identifiers: LCCN 2018011439 | ISBN 9780817017965 (pbk. : alk. paper)
Subjects: LCSH: Wealth—Religious aspects—Christianity—Sermons. | Economics—Religious aspects—Christianity—Sermons. | Christianity and justice—Sermons. | Reconciliation—Religious aspects—Christianity—Sermons.
Classification: LCC BR115.W4 E93 2018 | DDC 261.8/5--dc23 LC record available at https://lccn.loc.gov/2018011439

Printed in the U.S.A.
First printing, 2018.

Contents

Foreword

Judson Press is to be complimented for publishing *Reconciliation and Reparation: Preaching Economic Justice* by Joseph Evans. This is not just another book on the art and science of preaching. It is not another book on communication strategies, rhetorical styles, theologies of preaching, or a comparison of the sermons of celebrated modern-day preachers with the classical preaching masters of times past. This is not a feel-good book to read or a book to provide lazy preachers with ready-made sermons. This book will challenge contemporary preachers and interrogate the content of contemporary homiletics. This book is for the open-minded and for critical thinkers who are seeking to become twenty-first-century prophets.

Professors in the Academy of Homiletics will welcome this work by a critical interdisciplinary scholar and esteemed colleague whose expansive knowledge in homiletics, biblical exegesis, theology, philosophy, history, literature, economics, and ethics calls for a new hermeneutic and a new reading of the biblical narrative. Students of homiletics and seasoned preachers like myself will be inspired to rethink our motives for preaching and to examine what we have been doing, why we have been doing it, and what changes we need to make to be more effective preachers in the twenty-first century. Many of us have waited for another book like *Troubling Biblical Waters* edited by Cain Hope Felder and *Where Have All the Prophets Gone?* by Marvin A. McMickle. We need not wait longer. It is here. Joseph Evans has written it and Judson has published it.

The thesis of the book states that effective twenty-first-century preaching is prophetic when it proclaims an ethical imperative for followers of

Jesus of Nazareth to demand that those in power seek ways to close income and wealth gap. Now some may wonder why this is important. Readers who raise this question in thoughtful innocence would do well to study the preaching of the biblical prophets in Amos 3:6-16; 5:11-16; and Isaiah 1:21-27. Martin Luther King Jr. took the words of these prophets seriously. On May 11, 1959, in a conference with religious leaders at the Sheraton Park Hotel in Washington, DC, Dr. King said: "Any religion that professes to be concerned about the souls of men [and women] and is not concerned about the slums that damn them, the economic conditions that strangle them, and the social conditions that cripple them is a spiritually moribund religion, awaiting burial."

At this juncture Joseph Evans, in a very insightful way, introduces preachers to the Du Boisian prophetic tradition. This tradition is opaque to the mainstream; it is not normative conversation in the academy and church, and it is rarely mentioned in the preaching conferences that stage celebrity preachers. Another Judson Press author, Debra J. Mumford of Louisville Presbyterian Seminary, challenges the health-and-wealth gospel that allows churches to pursue self-centered, middle-class values that wed a religion of cheap grace to the so-called American dream. Dr. Mumford explores how this expression of prosperity religion affirms materialism to the neglect of racism, classism, sexism, militarism, and other forms of injustice. The Du Boisian prophetic tradition, which challenges European theological and cultural ideas and ideals, is also found in the writings of thinkers such as James Cone in his book *The Cross and The Lynching Tree* and in *Sisters in the Wilderness* from seminal womanist thinker Delores S. Williams. If there are still those who would vehemently contest the legitimate claims of the Du Boisian prophetic tradition as set forth by Evans, consider examining for yourself *The Africana Bible: Reading Israel's Scriptures from Africa and The African Diaspora*, Hugh R. Page, Jr., General Editor.[1]

Reconciliation in the Du Boisian thinking of Evans is no tearful kumbaya moment in front of a church campfire, but the making of amends for past sins. According to Evans the quest for economic justice is based on the foundations of the Poor People's Campaign, led by Dr. King calling for a fairer distribution of wealth. The contemporary poor are participants in the ongoing liberation struggle, and this struggle is global. We were not present at the table when reparations were given to the Jews for the holocaust. We were not at the table when Japanese Americans received reparations for their treatment in World War II, nor were we at the table when the Marshall Plan rebuilt Europe after that war. And no one laid a table at all for us after hundreds of years of black lives enslaved, oppressed, exploited, segregated, lynched, assaulted, shot unarmed, mass incarcerated, and unjustly accused. No reparations have been paid and America's bill is past due.

I highly recommend *Reconciliation and Reparation: Preaching Economic Justice* because the church must be the reconciling community, taking the initiative in bringing persons and nations everywhere to the table to talk to each other about the issues of justice.

J. Alfred Smith Sr.
Pastor Emeritus, Allen Temple Baptist Church
Professor Emeritus, American Baptist Seminary of the West

NOTE

1. Before any reader becomes nervous because Dr. Evans's work has a strong Africana perspective, let me highlight numerous white thinkers who share the ethical imperative for economic justice. They too preach a radicalized gospel in prophetic pulpits around the world. They too address income and wealth disparities. Let me introduce to you *Christology and Whiteness: What Would Jesus Do?* edited by George Yancy; *White Theology: Outing Supremacy in Modernity* by James W. Perkinson, *The Heart of Whiteness: Confronting Race, Racism, and White Privilege* by Robert Jensen; *The Wages of Whiteness: Race and the Making of the American Working Class* by David R. Roediger; *Divided by Faith: Evangelical Religion and the Problem of Race in America* by Michael O. Emerson and Christian Smith; *Dear White Christians: For Those Longing for Racial Reconciliation* by Jennifer Harvey; and *The End of White Christian America* by Robert P. Jones.

PART 1

Foundations

The Du Boisian
Prophetic Tradition

While attending the Progressive National Baptist Convention, USA, Inc.'s 2016 annual meeting, I left the Hyatt Regency hotel in New Orleans for my morning walk. From the hotel's front doors, located on Loyola Street, I walked out and turned right toward the Mississippi River, which bends around the city like a crescent—thus the Crescent City. After a short distance, Loyola intersects with Simon de Bolivar, a street named in honor of a great Latino political and military leader. Moving westward toward Louisiana, another intersecting street, I, who was once a student at one of the city's Baptist seminaries, became reacquainted with comforting smells of local chicory and coffee that complement the smell of fresh baking bread teeming from the Leidenheimer Baking Company.

Above the romantic sense of nostalgia, the streets appeared nearly the same as they did more than two decades ago. The blighted conditions remain constant, as though time had forgotten the people who made their homes in Mid-City, New Orleans. The experience led me to believe that post–Katrina New Orleans did not appear to be what many have called a post-racial era. Instead, it appeared to be similar to what I thought then and what I think now to be an economic caste system.

Now an infrequent visitor to New Orleans, I asked myself: "Where is the city's leadership's commitment to revitalize the Mid-City's family homes?" In my view, the old construct of race, economics, and politics continues to entangle people in poverty's barbwire. As I returned on

Simon de Bolivar, the large urban buildings, including the architectural spectacle of the Louisiana Superdome, were plainly in view. The experience was an ugly reminder: Poverty is tolerated in proximity with increasing, unrequited income and wealth inequalities.

The experience also helped me to bring clearly into view the thesis for this book; it came to life like a New Orleans morning filled with aromas: *Effective twenty-first-century preaching is prophetic when it addresses closing the income and wealth gap.* This economic gap can be closed but through deliberate means, which I define here as economic reparations. By this I mean economic restitution through financial redistribution. Throughout this book, I will make attempts to refine my definition for economic reparations, but for now it is important to introduce this concept as a key component for closing the economic gap, which is an income and wealth inequality.

Economist Thomas Piketty, the author of *Capital in the Twenty-First Century*, offers a compelling definition for income and wealth inequalities: "When the rate of return on capital exceeds the rate of growth of output and income, as it did in the nineteenth century and seems quite likely to do again in the twenty-first, capitalism automatically generates arbitrary and unstainable inequalities that radically undermine the meritocratic values in which democratic societies are based."[1] In short, Piketty argues that a corollary relationship must exist between meritocratic values and democracy. If this relationship fails to exists, there is little control over capitalism, which is another way to describe personal interest. Personal interest here points toward those who overwhelmingly have access to investment capital, and therefore the general welfare of societies and their sustainability are gravely threatened.

There are preachers who see similar contrasts between economic equalities and inequalities. For those of us who struggle with our calling to the prophetic tradition, this creates an internal and organic struggle to proclaim boldly, even to agitate for the necessary end of income and wealth inequalities, which is viewed widely as the controversial issue of this time.[2] Preachers, what is our starting point? One way to approach this daunting task is to critique what many have come to believe is our national collective biography, which I describe later in this chapter. For now, it is important to note that people who occupy different social locations more than likely intuitively interpret a collective biography differently than those who may affirm it through a Eurocentric lens. By a Eurocentric lens, I mean the dominant culture and its racial and class distinctions along with its worldview and hermeneutic grid.

These human conditions have compelled me to write this book as an attempt to disturb the status quo and cause meaningful, thoughtful conversations about a species of biblical preaching that envisions economic justice as the ethical imperative for the twenty-first century, particularly for people of African descent. It is written from a preacher's perspective that is informed by what I call the Du Boisian prophetic tradition. W. E. B. Du Bois, over his long career, focused on race, economics, and politics,[3] defining these as parts of Eurocentrism, the ideals of the dominant culture and class, and the idea that European cultural biases and values are premier.

When one follows the Du Boisian prophetic tradition, the worldview and hermeneutical lens of people of African descent then is employed for reading and understanding both secular and sacred texts and human interactions. In short, this approach seriously takes into consideration Du Bois's concept of double consciousness, which he defines as "One ever feels his twoness,—an American, a Negro; two souls, two thoughts, two unreconciled strivings; two warring ideals in one dark body, whose dogged strength alone keeps it from being torn asunder."[4] Furthermore, this tradition provides intellectual space for those who identify themselves in solidarity with people of African descent, and with people who are otherwise oppressed and living on the sociomargins. Because of this intellectual space and identification, preaching economic justice will emerge as relevant to many people who are looking for preachers to give them guiding hope.

A second reason for writing this book is to invite readers to participate in a meaningful and thoughtful debate about finally achieving the elusive goal of economic justice. By this, I mean that economic justice is a dogged and consummate pursuit of wealth and income equalities. Senator Bernie Sanders made this pursuit a focal point for his 2016 presidential candidacy: "America now has more wealth and income inequality than any major developed country on earth, and the gap between the very rich and everyone else is wider than at any time since the 1920s."[5] Sanders did not win the 2016 Democratic nomination, nor did the eventual Democratic Party nominee, Hillary Clinton, win the presidency, but Sanders's radicalized economic views continue to vibrate among many millennial radicalized activists.

A third reason for writing this book is a consideration of an ethical imperative for economic justice and what this imperative means for the twenty-first-century church and those who preach in prophetic pulpits around the world. Their impetus is that they are radicalized by the radicalized gospel. The church today can be named as the "World House," a phrase employed by Dr. Martin Luther King Jr.[6] By this, I mean a dogged and consummate pursuit of economic justice, which is another way to describe a pursuit of income and wealth equalities. These are Du Boisian preachers, people who are radicalized like King, who understood that this pursuit for equality clearly is a globalized mission. I contend, however, preachers of African descent must lead the way in part because there is a long-standing prophetic preaching tradition that may be traced to the nineteenth-century abolitionists and that this tradition continues well into the twenty-first century. This abolitionist's or preacher's view informed by the Du Boisian prophetic tradition can be traced directly to Martin Luther King Jr.

Writing in *Where Do We Go from Here: Chaos or Community?* King made a strong and prophetic statement that points toward a Christian community (his beloved community). Therein King appeals for human equality; this appeal indicates that all people must be a part of the "World House" which embraces that human equality is supported by achieving economic equality:

> Some years ago a famous novelist died. Among his papers was found a list of suggested plots for future stories, the most prominently underscored being this one: "A widely separated family inherits a house in which they have to live together." This is the great new problem of mankind. We have inherited a large house, a great "world house" in which we have to live together—black and white, Easterner and Westerner, Gentile and Jew, Catholic and Protestant, Muslim and Hindu—a family unduly separated in ideas, culture and interest, who, because we can never again live apart, must learn somehow to live with each other in peace.[7]

King, an exemplar of the Du Boisian prophetic tradition, was clear about the collective future of all people, which is influenced by our human experiences and environmental conditions. We come to know that all people are to be mutually respected regardless of our human identities. We who preach persuasive sermons that focus on texts that point toward economic justice are charged to make known that the World House is filled with people who embrace interdependence, and we identify with those who live on the sociomargins. Simply, this is a manifestation of Jesus of Nazareth's reign of God in the human realm. "Blessed are the poor in spirit, for theirs is the kingdom of heaven," Jesus said (Matthew 5:3, NASB).

All likeminded Christians and people of good will must answer King's call to the prophetic and in response doggedly pursue economic justice, and all must heed King's warning to those who benefit from Western cultural dominance and affluence. That dominance and affluence are at the taproot of the current global income and wealth imbalances which harshly affect much of the world's populations. We must remember that King pointed toward Western corporations and the like, making it clear that the oppressed are angry and resent their proximity to wealth and luxury and its rewards, and quite possibly like those who live in post–Katrina New Orleans, where their homes have not been restored. As mentioned earlier, towering above New Orleans Mid-City homes is that glaring symbol of income and wealth inequalities, the Superdome, a monument to capitalism gone awry. Because of these mutually shared global income and wealth inequalities and an unyielding, insensitive, and omnipresent Western materialism, many are trapped in degrading poverty.[8]

Democratic discussions need to occur about income and wealth inequalities that exist in our communities and in the world. For a large portion of the global population, many await realization of economic justice. We search then for results and solutions to achieve that goal. Economic justice discussions will emerge organically when preachers in the prophetic tradition proclaim that our pursuit of economic justice is our pursuit of wealth and income equalities. In addition, I contend that preachers in the prophetic tradition should consider Senator Sanders and his economic justice ideals and embrace his perspective as an allied guidepost in our fight to close the gap between "the very rich and everyone else," and "an economic gap wider than at any time since the 1920s."[9] These discussions precede solutions, and at the taproot of these discussions are preachers, women and men called to the prophetic tradition.

My claim here is that the twenty-first-century church's mantra is achieving economic justice. Preachers who are called to the prophetic tradition then are called to preach that economic justice is the word of reconciliation. Therefore, pulpiteers prophetically define that the motif of reconciliation is the dogged pursuit of economic justice, and indeed our pursuit is creating income and wealth equalities. What follows is a collective responsibility for societies, prompted by prophetic preaching from the church, which King called the World House, to eradicate human inequalities such as lack of adequate jobs, education and health care, clean water, food, adequate housing, immigration and criminal justice reform, and economic reparations for people of African descent globally.

These and other human inequalities are inconsistent with the ethical principles of Jesus of Nazareth and the kingdom of God in the human realm. In the following chapters, you as readers shall see that I employ exegesis of certain biblical passages that exemplify my claims. An immediate example, however, is that one has only to read about Jesus' miracle in which he feeds five thousand with a few barley loaves and fishes.[10] This miracle emphasizes a deliberate redistribution of resources so all who were present may live another day. If preachers do not respond as Jesus of Nazareth did, we will continue needlessly down a nihilistic path that leads to human unrest and wars, which is the cost of human life, and this is nothing less than irreparable damage.

I heard these principles echoed by Rev. Dr. Kevin Cosby, president of Simmons College. Cosby cited nearly verbatim a story that appeared in *The Nation* entitled "The Average Black Family Would Need 228 Years to Build the Wealth of a White Family Today." The author, Joshua Holland, wrote, "If the current economic trends continue, the average black household will need 228 years to accumulate as much wealth as their counterparts hold today. For the average Latino family, it will take 84 years. Absent significant policy interventions, or seismic change in the American economy, people of color will never close the gap."[11]

Holland's statistics and Cosby's sermon confirm the naked-eye test. For those who live in urban centers, one truly observes the tale of two cities. As far as the eye can see, the presence of emerging economic power is represented by gentrification: new building construction of all kinds, developing squarely in the face of a steadily declining presence of people of African descent in neighborhoods where these citizens have lived for generations.

Our Collective Cultural Biography

Cosby utilized published statistics that are disturbing. In fact, these statistics force us to reconsider the national collective biography. From my perspective, what should come under scrutiny is its interpretation because it is informed by Eurocentrism (meant here as a constant reinforcement of the dominant Western culture). Further, what is meant by these biases are systematic manipulations of race, economics, and politics. This unholy trinity underpins the Eurocentric model of the national collective biography. If we intend to eradicate this deliberate construct and achieve income and wealth equalities, it is necessary for us to make a first step.

Therefore, first, we start with reconsideration of our collective biography in the United States—that is, the depressing black and white narrative. Keep in mind, if there is one national narrative it is perceived to be the dominant culture's stories of rugged individualism, pulling oneself up by her or his bootstraps, personal freedom, unlimited opportunities, free markets, democracy, and capitalism, which is defined here as personal interest that may usurp public interest. Should these be imbalanced, the masses are subject to a privileged few who have access to investment and personal capital. It stands to reason that the narrative of people of African descent differs.

Thus, the interpretation of people of African descent differs from that informed by Eurocentrism. We take our lead from Du Bois. His textual interpretation does not depend on Eurocentric underpinnings. Du Boisian interpretation shapes different narrative species. His work is prophetic, and it is clear. That is, Du Bois deliberately creates a new narrative that points toward a different literary aesthetic for people of African descent. Described another way, Du Bois wanted people of African descent to employ something like his alternative aesthetic. By this I mean one that posits a "favorable form over function," which is an aesthetic. In this way and from this perspective, people do not gaze solely through a Eurocentric lens. Instead, Du Bois's invention casts a "black and blue" gaze, and through this one people see images of different heroes, heroines, subjects, and objects.

Take, for instance, James Baldwin, who is an heir to the Du Boisian prophetic tradition. Like Du Bois, Baldwin was a secular prophet who boldly proclaimed what he believed. A harsh critic of the Eurocentric narrative, Baldwin points out correctly that most people of African descent are suspicious of Eurocentric truth claims:

> The American Negro [and people of African descent wherever they may be located in the Diaspora] has the great advantage of having never believed the collection of myths to which white Americans cling: that their ancestors were all freedom-loving heroes, that they were born in the greatest country the world has ever seen, or that Americans are invincible in battle and wise in peace, that Americans have always dealt honourably with Mexicans and Indians and all other neighbours or inferiors, that American men are the world's most direct and virile, that American women are pure.[12]

As mentioned, Baldwin is an heir of the Du Boisian prophetic tradition. I reinforce this because Baldwin is certainly one of Du Bois's prophetic literary heirs. His talent is made evident by his masterful employment of written prose, appropriately arranged in powerful and lucid essay form. Baldwin's gift, however, is not located alone in his writing prowess. More than that, he was a courageous man who lifted the veil over Eurocentrism. Baldwin then counts among the prophetic seers.[13]

Like Du Bois, Baldwin focuses on hegemony that he locates in the Eurocentric narrative; and like Du Bois, Baldwin is suspicious of its flawed historicity, details that he associates with the claims of the dominant culture and classes' narrative. What of these questions: How do the oppressed respond to these would-be supremacy claims of the Eurocentric narrative? If only we had a pen, would we be heard? If we had intellectual space to cause meaningful and thoughtful discussions, conversations, and debates in the public and private spheres, spaces, and squares, would this lead to liberation for people of African descent and quite possibly for people of the dominant culture? How would the oppressed respond to what makes us equal in the public and private spheres, spaces, and squares?

I answer these questions in this way: Achieving income and wealth equalities has the potential to make us equal in public and private spheres, spaces, and squares. In fact, these are the only places people can be considered equal, which is, under the law. People cannot dictate equality to every human conscience and heart. Human equality, however, cannot be left to the dictates of our human hearts, which is better stated as human emotions. Some may know that like Du Bois and Baldwin, King was critical of those who idly stood by and did not ardently confront those who created, reinforced, and sustained Jim and Jane Crow culture. Instead, he wanted democratic and human rights to be reinforced by federal, state, and local laws, not Eurocentric culturally biased norms.[14] He thought it was the role of the radicalized church to inspire deconstruction of institutional spheres that were and are predominantly controlled by white elites.

In a similar fashion, preachers in the prophetic tradition must follow the Du Boisian model, as did Baldwin and King, and focus on the ethical mandates that we pursue. It is important to understand that achieving economic justice is achieving reconciliation. The claim to find reconciliation is simple to make but difficult to grasp for many black and white Eurocentric thinkers. Let us be clear: many are socially conditioned to believe that biblical reconciliation does not include economic justice. Readers will see later that indeed the apostle Paul's employment of the word *reconciliation* demands economic justice. Second Corinthians 5:20 is an example where the apostle Paul's employment of the word *reconciliation* is better translated to mean change or exchange; this is a legal phrase that is binding. It is not an emotional term referring to the human heart. What is claimed here is that twenty-first-century reconciliation is the word of economic justice. This means that there can be no authentic and lasting reconciliation without a change or exchange of resources that offers remedies for unjust inequalities. There can be no doubt: the last bastion of hegemonic power that hinders our efforts to achieve economic justice is wealth and income inequalities.

What comes next is something like the Du Boisian prophetic tradition which I have located in Baldwin's approach. Like his predecessor in this tradition, Baldwin sees Eurocentrism as a dysfunctional discourse that forms the dominant culture's national collective biography. If we assume that Baldwin's prose is prophetic and foretelling, we perceive he is correct, particularly because we see that his writing points to the underneath, the unsettling indicators about our current oppressive economic human conditions of "black and blue" people of African descent. This term "black and blue" refers to one of Louis Armstrong's most famous songs:

> Cold and empty bed, springs hard as lead
> Pains in my head, feel like old Ned
> What did I do to be so black and blue?
> No joys for me, no company
> Mouse ran from my house
> All my life through I've been so black and blue
> I'm white inside, but that don't help my case
> Cause I can't hide what is on my face
> I'm so forlorn. Life's just a thorn
> My heart is torn. Why was I born?
> What did I do to be so black and blue?[15]

Armstrong's song accurately describes the historical and current state of black America. We are a people who economically lag whites, minimally, for another 228 years. These statistics and facts point toward a daunting dose of reality. We cannot close this economic gap without deliberate and strategic interventions. I suggest that economic reparation is the only way to do so. If what I assert is true, it will take cooperation from all spectrums of our societies to confront the economic gap, which I have concluded is our income and wealth inequalities.

Preachers who are called to the Du Boisian prophetic tradition must grasp, understand, and accept this daunting reality. Then we are charged to explain this new perception of reality to our congregants and supporters. Also, Du Boisian preachers must anticipate resistance from stakeholders. Stakeholders are those who consciously and unconsciously defend and benefit financially because of Eurocentrism and its institutional spheres. You will recognize them because they are defenders of the status quo.

Du Boisian preachers must not be naïve about this looming confrontation. Instead, we are charged to proclaim that the ethical Jesus of Nazareth and his kingdom of God have come. It is our role to recognize and interpret his kingdom and point toward it for Christians and others. What is more, Du Boisian preachers believe that the kingdom of God is close to us. We believe this is true because we see that human equality, like the kingdom of God, is as near as our hands (Mark 1:15). Thus, we must imagine a world that embodies Jesus' ethical kingdom of God in the human realm, which I claim includes economic reparations. Reparations then point toward full economic equality in the institutional spheres. This can occur, but it requires an alternative narrative, a twenty-first-century corrective addition to our national collective biography. To be sure, there are consequences. It is a necessary price, however, that must be paid in order to see ourselves squarely. "The recovering alcoholic may well have to live with his illness the rest of his life. But at least he is not living a drunken lie. Reparations beckon us to reject the intoxication of hubris and see America as it is—the work of fallible humans."[16]

As the preceding excerpt shows, Ta-Nehisi Coates, the author of "The Case for Reparations," has made clear that narratives differ. Historically, the narrative of people of African descent questions the thesis of the dominant culture and then provides an antithesis, resulting in and settling for a new or at least a different synthesis. What is more, it focuses on the inaccuracies that pervade the former's storyline. Later in this chapter you will see that there is a difference between a storyline and a narrative. For now, it is important for us to focus on the failure of creating a new synthesis that does not lift the Veil Over Eurocentric supremacy claims.

A new synthesis then cannot remain inside of the proverbial Eurocentric cultural box. What I call the Eurocentric cultural box is similar to what Eddie Glaude Jr. calls the value gap. The value gap is the currency for retention of the status quo.[17] Thus the Eurocentric value gap does very little to change the human disadvantages which remain institutionally in place for people of African descent and other people. I contend that space must be made for other people's yearning for income and wealth equalities. A different metanarrative must emerge and be employed by preachers called to the Du Boisian prophetic tradition, those who will proclaim biblical truths for the twenty-first-century church.

A Different Metanarrative

Of course a narrative must be persuasive. Thus it has several parts that include compelling characters, settings, and major and minor plot-lines. Narrative, then, rises above current storylines, which too often are referred to as a narrative. By some this seems to be intentionally employed as misleading and manipulative demagoguery.

Instead, narrative belongs to many disciplines, but none are more important than psychology, literature, and history, all of which are present in the biblical writers' voices. In short, a narrative is a literary device that traces a subject's historical pathology. Expressed another way, narrative chronicles a subject's behavior over a historical time period.

The Birth of a Nation is a silent film (1915) that continues to excite mass audiences, surfaces a collective pathology, and reinforces a deep and abiding sense of racial superiority.[18] This notorious film should not be confused with Nate Parker's movie *The Birth of a Nation* (2016). About the earlier film, Parker remarks, "I've reclaimed this title and re-purposed it as a tool to challenge racism and white supremacy in America, to inspire a riotous disposition toward any and all injustice in this country (and abroad) and to promote the kind of honest confrontation that will galvanize our society toward healing and sustained systemic change."[19]

For another example that demonstrates that this collective pathology can be traced historically, we need only point toward an infamous South Carolina white woman named Susan Smith who in 1994 murdered her children and blamed a fictitious black man for the crime:

> Experts say the lies the 23-year-old mother [Susan Smith] told to cover her trail fit a long history of scapegoating black men for the ills of the nation. "This case demonstrates once again the stereotypical view of black men in America, that they are other, that they are dangerous, that they should be imprisoned," said Aldon Morris, who is black and the head of the sociology department at Northwestern University. "And this view, of course, is nothing new," he said. "It was the same view that guided lynch mobs during the days of segregation in the South. It is the same view that causes black men to be stopped, searched and harassed on a routine basis by the police."[20]

Smith was believed initially because she had tapped into a pathological mythology and into what makes a narrative a narrative: its common theme. What this precisely means is a narrative does not have to be true; it does have to be an accepted common cultural theme. It becomes a common cultural theme because its claims have been repeated so many times that those claims have been accepted to be true without critique or scrutiny. Thus the claim becomes culturally accepted but not necessarily true. In this context, what is repeated until it is believed to be true is both pathology and mythology. In the Smith case, it is about reinforcing into the psyche of a willing mass audience the notion that all black men are dangerous and all are capable of heinous acts which include murdering innocent children, especially white children.

Narratives, then, are made of stories, but these stories must be common themes: themes that point toward traceable pathologies. It is important here to make distinctions between the black and white pathologies that both inform and shape both narratives. From my view, the white narrative is the predominant narrative and can be characterized in the following ways: narratives of the oppressor and the oppressed, masters and slaves, colonizers and colonized. Whether rightly or wrongly, these narratives have shaped and informed the mainstream's pathologies which are normative in our American socioculture. The white narratives of supremacy have created a sense of inevitable greatness and a location of *ex cathedra*. The reinforced white narratives have effectively characterized people of African descent as inferior— and this is the dominant cultural message.

Indeed, the white narrative is not the only narrative, but it is the predominant one. It is predominating because it is reinforced and shaped as a Eurocentric construct. What is more, it is the Western culture's metanarrative because it is the predominantly known narrative that supersedes all others. This is a short definition for metanarrative, which we will discuss later in this chapter and throughout this book. The Eurocentric metanarrative best describes traditional Western culture's belief systems. These belief systems inform and shape the assumptions and applications of many disciplines, including efforts to preach biblical truth claims.

Like the Susan Smith story, the Eurocentric metanarrative provides, if not permits, only negative space for people of African descent and other people in nearly every private and public sphere, square, and space. Because of this, people of African descent are stereotyped and nearly invisible to the mainstream public, causing a virtual polarization in every human capacity. This does not lead to equality for people. So, how do we begin the healing process toward equality for people of all races, names, and faces?

I point toward a different metanarrative, one that speaks to a large segment of the world's populations. These majorities of people are sociologically oppressed, multicultural people, people of multi-colors, and people of African descent.

It is important to note here that any legitimate narrative is transparent and open for critique inside and outside of its boundaries. It is a necessary step toward the word of reconciliation, which I define as economic justice in two parts: income and wealth equalities. As mentioned earlier, economic justice is a remedy and, in addition, a public admission that white America's historic actions have injured people of African descent. Preaching economic justice from the perspective of people of African descent not only liberates masses of people of color; it also liberates all masses of people of all colors. In short, when people on the margins are liberated, then all people are liberated.

> This species of narrative is also a kind of counternarrative; it upsets the equilibrium of the establishment's status quo. In short, it confronts the limitations that the predominately Eurocentric metanarrative continues to posit. That is, its biased storylines which support hegemonic claims that suppress other hermeneutic, theological and rhetorical truth claims; these storylines . . . I further contend that these hegemonic claims support global economic oppression against people of color.[21]

This different metanarrative is necessary; it empowers us to move beyond Eurocentric hegemony.[22] The Du Boisian metanarrative, which is how we are naming that different metanarrative, is an attempt to embrace another person's presence and contributions to the human narrative, such as those contributed by people of African descent. Simply put, this different metanarrative is rooted in the black subject and is informed by an aesthetic that describes form and function that give shape to other perspectives. The Harlem Renaissance is an example of a literary revolution.

This revolution can be described as an effort to create a pan-African aesthetic. I believe this revolution was necessary to create intellectual and rhetorical space. The former enables preachers to reflect upon the black experience. The latter empowers preachers' rhetorical space to share the black experience. Readers, please keep in mind that an aesthetic is the point of departure for developing such intellectual and rhetorical space. An aesthetic then is a device which forms narrative and guides its functions.

Second, this different metanarrative embraces pan-Africanism, which is a philosophical point of departure. For example, Molefi Kete Asante, who is an influential pan-Africanist scholar, defines an economic justice motif as a word of reconciliation, but in the following way:

> The argument for reparations for forced enslavement of Africans in the American colonies and the United States of America is based in moral, legal, economic, and political grounds. Taken together these ideas constitute an enormous warrant for the payment of reparations to the descendants of the Africans who worked under duress for nearly 250 years. The only remedy for such an immense deprivation of life and liberty is an enormous restitution.[23]

Asante brilliantly defines economic justice in four parts: moral, legal, economic, and political grounds. Together these are economic restitution: "Recognizing that justice may be both retributive and restorative, it seeks to punish those who have committed wrong and it concerns itself with restoring to the body politic a sense of reconciliation and harmony."[24] Asante, however, leans toward the latter, namely, that economic justice is restorative.

I, however, see retributive as irreplaceable. Asante himself has grounded his claim for reparations in the institutional sphere of the courts, which is another way of describing by legal means. Courts are supposed to decide on the facts and render justice with punitive consequences to deter further illegal behavior, lest it become an unaccepted cultural norm. Thus, justice is also judgment. Both are redemptive, and therefore some of the chapters in this book may be characterized as a type of judgment which one hopes will lead to restorative steps toward healing people of African descent and the global community.[25]

Third, this different metanarrative, which I identify with the Du Boisian prophetic tradition, invents its own subjects which are significant features for narrative development. Namely, people of African descent are the heroes and heroines and collective symbols of our narrative which historically traces our own pathologies and further helps us to explain why, how, and what shapes our behavioral development.

Conclusion

If we are to be effective twenty-first-century preachers, we must be serious about calling forth economic justice, bringing to pass income and wealth equalities. Thus, we listen to compatible voices—clear voices that dare to try and reach the most difficult prophetic registers. These voices are clear because they have tapped into our ethical imperative, which is agitating for economic justice. I contend those who agitate for economic justice are among the seers in the Du Boisian prophetic tradition. We refuse to abandon Jesus' vision of the kingdom of God in our human realm. Preachers, however, must redefine the Lord's church to mean that the entire body of Christ understands that all people are equal and desire to be humanized and are valued partners; parts of a whole, which is our global community.

Finally, preachers in the Du Boisian prophetic tradition believe that this different metanarrative, the metanarrative of African descent, will be the window into the souls of sociomarginalized people everywhere. The Du Boisian metanarrative is made of stories of liberation and democratic yearnings that we believe manifest guiding hope. We envision income and wealth equalities, the two parts of economic justice, which I believe breaks down human barriers and false senses of human superiorities. To achieve this laudatory goal, Du Boisian preachers are willing to listen to voices inside and outside of our ecclesial institutions (which I will address in a later chapter) to those who share our common goal to achieve economic justice. Our common thread is to create a different consciousness.

Du Boisian preachers then are radicalized by the gospel of Jesus of Nazareth and seek righteousness and justice so that our souls may be soothed. Du Boisian preachers seek to preach for the formation of these soothed souls, but first we must preach to form a different kind of consciousness inside and outside of the communities of people of African descent, consciousness that will move us onward. We recognize that people of good will come from many places, and we must embrace their sincerities as far as they may be sincere and willing to travel this arduous path with us.

In the end, readers will find that our travels will intersect in similar spaces and places. Preachers in this prophetic tradition as we define it (as in the tradition of the biblical prophets of old) will be often misunderstood. We will rub some people the wrong way for myriad reasons, some of which are found in the content of this book. But we preach economic justice because we are compelled to do so by Jesus of Nazareth, and therefore we can do no other.

NOTES

1. Thomas Piketty, *Capital in the Twenty-First Century*, trans. Arthur Goldhanmmer (Cambridge, MA: The Belknap Press of Harvard University Press, 2014), 1.

2. Ibid., 2–3.

3. W. E. B. Du Bois, *Dusk of Dawn: An Essay Toward an Autobiography of a Race Concept* (Piscataway, NJ: Transaction Publishers, 2011), 47.

4. W. E. B. Du Bois, *The Souls of Black Folk* (New York: Bantam Books, 2005), 3.

5. See Bernie Sanders, "Income and Wealth Inequality," https://bernie sanders.com/issues/income-and-wealth-inequality/, accessed December 15, 2016.

6. See Martin Luther King Jr., *Where Do We Go from Here: Chaos or Community?* (Boston: Beacon Press, 1968).

7. Martin Luther King Jr., "The World House," in *The Radical King*, ed. Cornel West (Boston: Beacon Press, 2015), 75.

8. Ibid., 82.

9. Sanders, "Income and Wealth Inequality."

10. See John 6:1-14, NASB.

11. Joshua Holland, "The Average Black Family Would Need 228 Years to Build the Wealth of a White Family Today," *The Nation* (August 8, 2016), https://www.thenation.com/article/the-average-black-family-would-need-228-years-to-build-the-wealth-of-a-white-family-today/, accessed December 5, 2016.

12. James Baldwin, *The Fire Next Time* (New York: The Modern Library, 1995), 100.

13. Joseph Evans, *Lifting the Veil Over Eurocentrism: The Du Boisian Hermeneutic of Double Consciousness* (Trenton, NJ: Africa World Press, 2014), 10.

14. Martin Luther King, Jr., "The World House" in *The Radical King*, ed. Cornel West (Boston: Beacon Press, 2015), 83–84.

15. Louis Armstrong, *The Great Chicago Concert 1956—Complete* (Columbia Legacy, 1956).

16. Ta-Nehisi Coates, "The Case for Reparations," *Atlantic* (June 2014), 57.

17. See Eddie Glaude Jr., *Democracy in Black: How Race Still Enslaves the American Soul* (New York: Crown Publishers, 2016), 6.

18. Melvyn Stokes, *D.W. Griffith's "The Birth of a Nation": A History of "The Most Controversial Motion Picture of All Time"* (Oxford: Oxford University Press, 2008).

19. Wikipedia, citing Soheil Rezayazdi (January 25, 2016), "Five Questions with the *Birth of a Nation* Director Nate Parker," *Filmmaker*.

20. Don Terry, "A Woman's False Accusations Pains Many Blacks," *New York Times* (November 6, 1994), http://www.nytimes.com/1994/11/06/us/a-woman-s-false-accusation-pains-many-blacks.html, accessed December 5, 2016.

21. Joseph Evans, "The Radical Nature of the Du Boisian Metanarrative and Economic Reparations," *Homiletic* 41, no. 1 (2016), 4.

22. Evans, *Lifting the Veil*, 161.

23. Molefi Kete Asante, "The African American Warrant for Reparations: The Crime of European Enslavement of Africans and Its Consequences," in *Should America Pay? Slavery and the Raging Debate on Reparations*, ed. Raymond A. Winbush (New York: Amistad, 2003), 4.

24. Ibid., 5.

25. Ibid.

CHAPTER 2

Our Poor People's Campaign
Our Liberation March and
Liberation Narrative

The Poor People's Campaign mobilization had driven King to the nadir of his public career and his consequent assassination at Memphis. Few people outside of the King family circle know that Dr. King's widow [Coretta Scott King] recruited this writer to handle the logistics and management details for Dr. King's funeral services in Atlanta.[1] –Wyatt Tee Walker

In the fall of 1951, Wyatt Tee Walker and Martin Luther King Jr. met on the Virginia Union University campus. Both men were sons of preachers and presidents of their respective seminary classes:

> The first time I met Martin Luther King Jr. was on the campus of Virginia Union University in Richmond, Virginia. King was a senior graduate student at Crozier Seminary, then located in Chester, Pennsylvania, about twelve miles south of Philadelphia. As president of the student body at Crozier, he was one of two delegates attending the Middle Atlantic regional meeting of the Interseminary Movement and the Graduate School of VUU was the host campus in the early fall of 1951. ISM was a quasi-artificial organization that provided an opportunity for ministers-in-training in the South to meet and fraternize without risk of arrest *for whites and blacks being together in public assembly.* My direct contact with Martin Luther King Jr. was a result of this writer

serving as president of the seminary student body despite the fact I was only a Middler.[2]

Indeed Walker and King's initial meeting was inspired and became a lifelong mutual love, respect, and friendship. This was nothing less than providential; it set the course for our liberation march that included economic boycotts to irritate and dismantle Southern power structures that eventually changed the American South's homogenous-segregation culture. "From 1960 to 1964, Walker served as chief of staff to the Rev. Martin Luther King Jr. and executive director of the Southern Christian Leadership Conference [SCLC], the civil rights organization headed by King. Walker was a key adviser on structure and strategy, helping develop, for example, the SCLC's watershed 1963 campaign in Birmingham, Alabama. King called him 'one of the keenest minds of the nonviolent revolution.'"[3] These early struggles are significant events of the liberation march—events which continue, shaping the contours of what I call our liberation narrative.

This narrative becomes highly visible when it is considered alongside Dr. Walker's and Dr. King's movement that led to the historic Poor People's Campaign. We shall see later in this chapter that this campaign was gravely hindered because of King's assassination. Still, the campaign was a part of a nearly decade-long civil rights strategy to achieve human rights which I have defined as income and wealth equalities (economic justice). Again, this human-radicalized transformation points toward the oppressed and sociomarginalized citizens in general, and specifically it points toward people of African descent in America. Because we know that the need for transformation continues, I have renamed it our poor people's campaign.

In the previous chapter, I tried to shape this emerging liberation narrative by suggesting that it is informed by our contemporary understanding of reconciliation. We continue, then, our dogged pursuit toward our noble goal. It is reemphasized here that income and wealth equalities are significant parts that define human rights. This is what lay at the heart of this book's thesis: *Effective twenty-first-century preaching is prophetic when it addresses closing the income and wealth gap.*

To further advance our contemporary application of the word of reconciliation, it is fitting and necessary to bring into focus our historical march toward black liberation. In short, the liberation march remains our collective pursuit, and it serves as our point of departure to describe what shapes the contours of our liberation narrative. The liberation narrative reinforces the prophetic preaching of people of African descent, which I have defined as preaching in the Du Boisian prophetic tradition.

Most prophetic preaching occurs in worship and that within assemblies of people. Thus, we can refine our thesis by tracing it to our longest-serving visible institution, namely, the church of people of African descent. Historically, the church has been our stabilizing force, our advocate, and our agitator. The black church has produced some of the most attractive and familiar figures in American sociohistory. Later in this chapter, I will rely on Wyatt Tee Walker's memories of the civil rights campaigns and introduce readers to the close relationship Wyatt Tee Walker shared with Martin Luther King Jr. For now, it is important to reconsider the historical role that the black church (I refer to the black church interchangeably with the church of people of African descent) has had and continues to produce a black leadership class from within the church at large.

Black church history is too rich, too broad, and too complex to recite here. Readers, however, will benefit from a brief sociohistorical sketch. There are no sociologists or historians who have made larger contributions to aid our understanding of the role and origin of the black church than E. Franklin Frazier and C. Eric Lincoln. Their magisterial works were published as two volumes in a single book called *The Negro Church in America and The Black Church Since Frazier*. Both scholars greatly formed and shaped the contours of our liberation narrative.

Frazier writes original texts, and Lincoln builds on Frazier's contributions by including what were then current writings by civil rights and post–civil rights activists and authors. I claim these writers were heirs of the Du Boisian prophetic tradition. By contrast, we will soon see that through Lincoln's "Introduction," he explains what had occurred socially ten years after Frazier published *The Negro Church in America*. That is, the Negro church had evolved into a black church. In part, he does this by tracing the evolution as an ongoing sociohistory. For now, we turn toward E. Franklin Frazier's work.

E. Franklin Frazier: The Sustaining
Negro Church and Culture

E. Franklin Frazier's *The Negro Church in America* begins with the "Religion of the Slaves." What is of import here is that Franklin courageously paints a tawdry portrayal of social terrorism. If terrorism is successful, its goal is to annihilate people's cultural roots and eventually to destroy the presence of an entire racial construct:

> In studying any phase of the character and the development of the social and cultural life of the Negro in the United States, one must recognize from the beginning that because of the manner in which the Negroes were captured in Africa and enslaved, they were practically stripped of their social heritage [and economic viability]. Although the area in West Africa from which the majority of slaves were drawn exhibits a high degree of cultural homogeneity, the capture of many of the slaves in intertribal wars and their selection for the slave markets tended to reduce to a minimum the possibility of the retention and the transmission of African culture. The slaves captured in the intertribal wars were generally males and those selected for the slave markets on the African coasts were the young and the most vigorous. This was all in accordance with the demands of the slave markets in the New World.[4]

Frazier's scholarship describes horrific experiences which express nothing less than Western, cultural, market-driven terrorism. It is terrorist activism that continues to impose itself upon the psyche of people of African descent and, in this instance, those who are children of American slaves. As the descendants of African slaves, we have (until Barack Obama) carried an unbearable cultural stigma. What is more, these hegemonic cultural practices are seedbeds and proponents for continuous unjust and inhumane laws, and specifically laws that punish people of African descent socioeconomically. We lag people of Eurocentric descent in nearly every measurable sociocategory.

Frazier is compelling because he has made all aware that people of African descent have endured forcible separation from our physical boundaries, family structures, cultural myths, and religions. We are people who have been and continue to be manipulated sociopsychologically; we are people who have been and continue to be among the first of many people denied our human rights to self-identities on American soil. The lack of self-identities severely impairs any sense of nationalistic patriotism and social cohesion: "The enslavement of the Negro not only destroyed the traditional African system of kinship and other forms of organized social life but it made insecure and precarious the most elementary form of social life which tended to sprout anew, so to speak, on American soil—the family."[5]

Indeed, this burden is caused by a materialized empire which feeds itself through exploitation and manipulation. We know for certain, this burden is ongoing and borne disproportionately by the oppressed. Of the degradations mentioned the most egregious terrorist act results in what appears to be a deliberate disintegration of the families of people of African descent. "There was, of course, no legal marriage and the relation of the husband and father to his wife and children was a temporary relationship dependent upon the will of the white masters and the exigencies of the plantation régime."[6] The "plantation regime" is another name for empire.

Empire then serves as the antagonist for the birth of the church of people of African descent. Our church is the protagonist which has multiple roles, which includes the formation of a religious, social, economic, and psychological institution. At its inception, our church attempts to preserve our community's human dignity.[7] It too serves as our collective, visible repairer of our total human breach. In short, the church of people of African descent helps to sustain our communal survival. To survive exploitation and manipulation is to resist hegemonic power that historically people of African descent have associated with dominating culture and classes and its narrative. It is this Eurocentric narrative that undergirds empire.

Until now, we have not made any clear distinction between Frazier's characterizations of the Negro and his "Negro Church," which socially parallels Negro culture and narrative. As mentioned earlier, some of my content may offend some of our most gentle readers' spirits. Still, it is necessary to risk offending some to inform others why the Negro church, its culture, and its narrative have evolved into a "church of African descent," its culture, and its liberation narrative.

Here, the Negro is a compliant person who has perfected emulation, if not adoring belief, in the superiority of the Eurocentric church, its culture, and its dominating narrative. This emulation can be labeled today as Negro pathology, which is another way to describe a person or persons who have not developed self-determined identities. Because of this, the Eurocentric narrative is a harmfully destructive psychological phenomenon which, too often, is located in the so-called Negro's daily life.[8] The phenomenon is a psychosocial construct with psychospiritual implications which manifests degradation and a lack of self-determined identities among people of African descent. This pathology is what Henry Louis Gates calls the signifying monkey.[9] Negro pathology then is that which looks for approval from the white power structure.

Negro pathology is seen in the current economic interests of African American political leaders, at least in those who appear to be devoid of true self-consciousness, the result of double consciousness. This is at the taproot of W. E. B. Du Bois's definition: "One ever feels his [her] twoness,—an American, a Negro; two souls, two thoughts, two unreconciled strivings; two warring ideals in one dark body, whose dogged strength alone keeps it from being torn asunder."[10] Many Congressional Black Caucus members, for example, pledged their unyielding support to Hillary Clinton's 2016 presidential bid against Donald Trump instead of to Senator Bernie Sanders. This was misguided trust.

Ironically, Senator Sanders's policies are similar to human rights motifs shared by radicalized people of African descent. Sanders's policies support our human rights agenda. Sanders's policies include single payer universal healthcare and the dismantling of Wall Street economic power, which means breaking up large banking monopolies that serve plutocratic and oligarchical economic interests. Among his policies is his acknowledgment that immigration and incarceration reform must include restoration of full citizenship rights for people of African descent. Too often, people of African descent have not recovered their right to vote, which epitomizes full citizenship rights. It must be mentioned, Terry McAuliffe, then governor of Virginia, restored former felons their right to vote in 2016 during the presidential campaign.

Another clear example of Negro pathology is film moguls and actors who capitulate to materialism to make television shows such as *Scandal*, *Empire*, and *Black-ish*, which are redux of *The Jeffersons* and *The Cosby Show* from the 1970s and the 1980s. These sitcoms are offensive to radicalized people of African descent because they reinforce stereotypical characterizations. In short, too often we are portrayed as docile, tragicomedic people. Of course this characterization serves to reinforce white power structures. This further reinforces the psychological enslavement which undergirds Negro pathology. By contrast, in the middle 1960s we saw an intellectual class who embraced their Africanism and rhetorically began to move away from Negro pathology toward a pan-African ideology which is definitively Du Boisian. Equally important to our definition, pan-African ideology births a new black self-consciousness. This evolved into a nationalistic call for Black Power. In short, Black Power demands human rights.

Black Power signifies a pan-African ideology which emerged rhetorically from the lips of Stokely Carmichael. Carmichael was a civil rights leader associated with the Student Nonviolent Coordinating Committee (SNCC). He uttered the phrase during a rally in Greenwood, Mississippi, on June 16, 1966. The phrase "Black Power" was both cathartic and prophetic. "The only way we gonna stop the white men from whuppin' us is to take over. We have been saying freedom for six years and we ain't got nothin'. What we gonna start saying now is Black Power!"[11]

> I raised the call for Black Power again. It was nothing new; we'd been talking about nothing else in the Delta for years. The only difference was that this time the national media was there. And most of them had never experienced the passion and fervor of a mass meeting before. As I passed Mukasa [Willie Ricks], he said, "Drop it now. The people are ready. Drop it now."[12]

Black Power symbolizes that which has occurred, namely, a cultural (narrative) paradigm shift. It further means that people of African descent began to understand that our liberation march must have its own liberation narrative. A narrative that belongs to people of African descent is employed to tell our story, using a rhetorical strategy that creates the black subject. The black subject resists objectification. To advocate for human rights is to know first that we are human and equally so with everyone else. In short, this means a change of psychological consciousness. To further define the term, we point toward Amos N. Wilson's lengthy but necessary explanation:

> Consciousness is a psychological control mechanism. It is an instrument of behavioral control. Through its states and levels [of being], humans control their mental, physical and emotional behavior. However, consciousness can be socialized, meaning that its defining functional contents—methods of processing and expressing information, its guiding values and parameters—are deeply influenced and conditioned by the nature of consistency of or interactions with other human beings and various social conditions under which we live. In other words, the consciousness that directs the individual's behavior is to a great degree under social control, and used as a means of controlling his [and her] behavior by the culture, society, groups of which he [and she] is a member and under social control. Consequently, its contents, character, abilities and intentions are the objects of social concern and social engineering. To control consciousness is to control behavior or at least, to limit its possibilities.[13]

What is of import here is that Wilson, another heir of the Du Boisian prophetic tradition, makes clear that Black Power is psychologically and socially a state of self-consciousness. As previously mentioned, people of African descent cannot demand our human rights, which is income and wealth equalities, unless we can sociopsychologically transcend the dominating culture and class and its narrative. For too long the Eurocentric narrative has reinforced the obscure notion that people of African descent do not deserve economic equality. Thus, Black Power is first a sociopsychological point of departure.

This analysis may have been unsettling to some but necessary to inform all. Social change and progress are never neat and tidy. My intention then is to explain the social dynamics that have occurred and led to our evolution from the Negro church, culture, and narrative toward the black church and its culture and liberation narrative. This brief characterization that I have unlordly employed is to provide context to C. Eric Lincoln's scholarly work. In this way, we now turn toward Lincoln's analysis, which traces our aforementioned social change and progress. In short, this explains our liberation march from the Negro church toward the black church.

C. Eric Lincoln: The Emergence of the Church of People of African Descent and Culture

We begin by paying close attention to Lincoln's "Introduction," which provides some explanation for Lincoln's approach to our enormous task. The substantial excerpt that follows aids us in our effort to trace the sociohistorical differences which took place over a short period of time:

> It was roughly twenty years ago that E. Franklin Frazier first conceived his "Evolution of Religion Among American Negroes" as the Frazier Liverpool Lecture in Social Anthropology at the University of Liverpool. It has been only ten years since the Frazier Lecture, augmented with new materials and refocused to treat specifically "the role of religion in the social organization of Negro life in the United States," emerged as *The Negro Church in America*. Ten years is a short time in which to measure "change" in the area of religious practices. Religion, like law, by its very nature and by the ultimate implications of its meaning for its practitioners, is not expected to register change with every shift of the wind in the ongoing life of the community. Indeed, it is the stability of religion, its tradition of endurance, its transcendence of social flux which enables men [and women] to find in it the security and assurance they need to rescue them for the meaninglessness of change *qua* change. When the "invisible institution" sang of that "Old-time Religion," its reference was to a kind of religion remembered for its faithfulness and consistency. It was a religion which had been tried and proven worthy of the testimonials of time.[14]

Lincoln delimits his analysis, admitting that only ten years had passed since Frazier's *The Negro Church in America*. In addition, he concedes that "religion, like law, by its very nature and by the ultimate implications of its meaning for its practitioners, is not expected to register change with every shift of the wind in the ongoing life of the community."[15] In this way, Lincoln points his readers' expectations toward religion that changes slowly, and it usually marks time before it gradually changes. Nevertheless, he points toward those gradual changes that parallel an evolving society and particularly changes that are noticed in the sociocultural practices and expectations of people of

African descent in America. Perhaps the most significant change in our religious practices is our focus on emerging human rights.

This becomes evident when we consider that Lincoln's first chapter is "Black Power: A Statement by the National Committee of Negro Churchmen." The manifesto was collectively written by self-described "Negro churchmen in America." I recast them here as heirs of the Du Boisian prophetic tradition:

> We an informal group of Negro Churchmen in America, are deeply disturbed about the crisis brought upon our country by historic distortions of important human realities in the controversy about "black power." What we see shining through the variety of rhetoric is not anything new but the same old problem of power and race which has faced our beloved country since 1619.[16]

The year 1619 is a significant marker. It signifies time and distance traveled by disenfranchised people of African descent, and secondly it signifies that the Du Boisian writers have set rhetorical boundaries. Readers then can locate these writers' point of departure and notice that 1619 serves as the aegis for our liberation march and narrative. Also, the year 1619 is symbolic; it is employed to demand full democratic human rights (income and wealth equalities).

Thus the year 1619 indicates human rights have long been coming and are now demanded. It was that year that the colony of Jamestown was established. That same year, historians recorded the presence of African slaves on Virginian soil at Jamestown. The Du Boisian writers' narrative rhetorical strategy then is to employ symbols that connect ideas with language—language employed to connect the controversy over white power sharing with the lack of self-determining agency among people of African descent.[17] What follows are three aspects of these Du Boisian preachers' rhetorical strategy, a strategy that is informed by a liberation narrative for people of African descent.

The liberation narrative's first claim is that our human rights struggle began our movement. It further describes that the movement began the exact moment the bondsmen and women placed their feet onto our American shores. Sadly, what began others' American dream paradoxically began our American nightmare. The year 1619 surfaces undemocratic and economic suffering experienced by people of African descent. By comparison, white settlers pursued democratic rights and freedom from European class tyranny. White settlers, however, intentionally kept those same democratic rights and independence from people of African descent (as well as Native Americans).

The Du Boisian writers suggest that the story of people of African descent began at Jamestown but evolved into our liberation narrative. We can imagine the differences between the dominating narrative and that of people of African descent. The former narrative describes heroic founders without reference to their denial of others' humanity and human rights. The latter describes that despite these denials, our heroic founders endured the white settlers' unfair treatment which may have led to annihilation. Indeed, these people of African descent survived genocidal extinction. The key signifier here is "the same old problem of power and race which has faced our beloved country since 1619."[18] This is a powerful statement which further helps us to shape the contours of our liberation narrative, which is to achieve human rights.

A second aspect of the liberation narrative is its rhetorical strategy which links and connects terms that make the rhetorical argument plausible. Chaim Perelman's work on how symbols function and connect relationships between ideas, persuasion, and conviction parallels what these writers have done.[19] That is, these Du Boisian writers have connected symbols to make their claims persuasive. If Perelman is to be taken seriously, then we accept there is an equal relationship between "black power" and "Christian conscience." Thus, our intention is to suggest that the Du Boisian writers have made plausible moral and legal clams which are justifications for human rights.

What is more, these Du Boisian writers argue subtly that the former is equal to the latter, and therefore readers are asked to accept that "black power" is another expression of democratic rights, protected by America's founding documents and in this instance, the third article of the United States Bill of Rights: "Congress shall make no law respecting an establishment of religion, or prohibiting the free exercise thereof; or abridging the freedom of speech, or of the press; or the right of the people peaceably to assemble, and to petition the Government for a redress of grievances."[20] This rhetorical move is strategic because it links "black power" with our constitutionally guaranteed free exercise of speech and a petition to the United

States federal government for "redress of grievances." In this way, "black power" and "Christian conscience" are connected and equally valued. That is, people of African descent are revolutionaries in their time as the founding patriots were during the Revolutionary War period.

A third aspect of the liberation narrative's rhetorical strategy is an adept use of syllogisms to make an equality argument, suggesting first that both blacks' and whites' concept of self is distorted by an unhealthy distribution of economic power. This distortion includes an "absence of justice" which results in a skewed expression of love and "becomes chaotic self-surrender." It is precisely the latter that motivates the Du Boisian writers. Self-surrender is a part of the so-called Negro pathology. Indeed, it is this negative part of the "Negro" narrative. Thus it became necessary for these Du Boisian writers and preachers to change the narrative by addressing existing pathologies. What emerged was a liberation narrative that is informed by a pan-African ideology. This new liberation narrative empowered people of African descent to claim our history, but we reserve the right to revise our narrative as more light is shined upon our path.

Indeed, people of African descent began to move from powerlessness toward power. In short, power was necessary to refine our march toward liberation; we became the subject of our narrative by claiming that we demanded human rights, which explain the euphemism black power. This is plausible. These Du Boisian writers were correct when they expressed that people of Africa descent had no power "to implement the demands of conscience." By contrast, people of non-color possessed conscienceless power, and therefore these writers claimed, "We are faced now with a situation where conscienceless power meets powerless conscience, threatening the very foundation of our nation."[21]

The paradox of power and powerlessness frames what can be thought of as a nihilistic dilemma—an impasse of sorts.[22] From this perspective, these writers' task becomes our task, which is to fight against a growing threat of hopelessness and fatalistic tendencies that have successfully kept the psyche of Negro in isolation—life within the veil, which further relegates him and her into "something" soulless. What is necessary for people of African descent then is to create a new cultural paradigm, a new way of thinking for ourselves and engaging, if not educating, the broader public that what is taking place is a psychospiritual transformation. In other words, the newly radicalized have tapped into a new power; indeed, a power for deconstructing the psyche of the Negro and replacing the fossilized Negro psyche with the psyche of a radicalized people of African descent.

Lincoln's task was clear. He began his study with that which then currently informed the social fabric and the communal life of people of African descent which was rapidly moving toward an independent self-definition—that is, what it means to be black and committed to self-determinism. These Du Boisian preachers were a part of that movement and represented the masses by continuing to refine our liberation narrative:

> We realize that neither the term "power" nor the term "Christian Conscience" is an easy matter to talk about, especially in the context of race relations in America. The fundamental distortion facing us in the controversy about "black power" is rooted in a gross imbalance of power and conscience between Negroes and white Americans. It is this distortion, mainly, which is responsible for the widespread, though often inarticulate, assumption that white people are justified in getting what they want through the use of power, but that Negro Americans must, either by nature or by circumstances, make their appeal only through conscience. As a result, the power of white men and the conscience of black men have both been corrupted. The power of white men is corrupted because it meets little meaningful resistance from Negroes to temper it and keep white men from aping God. The conscience of black men is corrupted because, having no power to implement demands of conscience, the concern for justice is transmuted into a distorted form of love, which, in the absence of justice, becomes chaotic self-surrender. Powerlessness breeds a race of beggars. We are faced now with a situation where conscienceless power meets powerless conscience, threating the foundations of our nation.[23]

What have these writers expressed? Black power is an autonomous alternative to Eurocentrism. Black power then is a conscious state of being. It is a psychospiritual baptism that results in radicalized converts who are defiant and resist forms of hegemonic structures of oppression, and in this instance, hegemonic structures that are supported by the Eurocentric (meta)narrative. We return to Wilson to further refine our definition and what it means to be baptized into the black power movement and converted into a new consciousness that our informs liberation narrative:

> To possess consciousness is to be possessed by consciousness. For consciousness "takes over" and represents itself in the body as feelings, emotions, tastes, values, intelligence, and behavior. When relatively stable or consistent, habitual dispositions and tendencies which dynamically structure and are reciprocally structured by consciousness, incline the individual or group to act or react in certain fairly predictable ways. . . . The related tendencies which characterize an individual's consciousness conjoin to generate practices, perceptions, and attitudes which may appear to the individual and others to be natural, cultural, or compulsive in nature.[24]

What Wilson describes is an intellectual conversion. New converts have formed a radicalized consciousness, and we sense that self-sacrifice is necessary to reach our goals of liberation. This radicalization is similar to that which possessed Jesus and his disciples. "If any want to become my followers, let them deny themselves and take up their cross and follow me. For those who want to save their life will lose it, and those who lose their life for my sake, and for the sake of the gospel, will save it" (Mark 8:34-35, NRSV). Radicalized disciples are those who are possessed by a radicalized consciousness, and we are in solidarity to dismantle oppressive systems. This is similar to what Du Boisian preachers prophetically advocate in prophetic-leaning churches of people of African descent.

Although the collective church of African descent has diverse polities and theological praxis, it is our sustaining catalyst. We are people faced with racial bigotries and intellectual biases. Still, predominately, we are people committed to human progress. Without incessant progress, people of African descent will continue to face their looming and largest existential challenge, which is quite literally psychological if not physical annihilation.

To threaten the existence of any people is an abuse of power. This threat has been used successfully to hinder, if not prevent, our progression toward human rights. As mentioned earlier, we cannot rehearse our liberation march entirely. Instead, our liberation march is viewed narrowly by my employment of attractive and familiar figures that embody our ongoing struggle toward human rights. Since 1619, this is justice pursued doggedly by people of African descent. Our account begins with my revision of the modern civil rights movement. I attempt here to do so by focusing on our poor people's campaign. The poor people's campaign continues to be significant because it dramatizes the evolution and emergent nature of our liberation narrative. Wyatt Tee Walker was an attractive figure who further shaped our liberation narrative.

Wyatt Tee Walker: "A First-Person, Eye-Witness Account"[25]

Like others mentioned in this chapter, Wyatt Tee Walker was an heir of the Du Boisian prophetic tradition. He was the author of many published books, essays, and articles. Walker's magisterial work, however, had not been finished. He titled the draft *The King of Love: My Days with Martin Luther King Jr*. I interviewed Walker, and excerpts of that interview were published in "Let Wyatt Handle This" in the *University of Richmond Magazine*. I asked Walker why he had not finished *The King of Love*. He replied, "I think part of it was the awe that I maintained for Dr. King, that I didn't feel I was ready. I still think I need to write about him sometime because I was very close to him, and I had many, many, many conversations with him."[26] Walker was an intimate friend to King and an eyewitness to the events that surrounded the martyred civil rights leader and Baptist preacher. At the same time Walker was the architect for the strategically planned and organized resistance campaign to Jim Crow and segregation. Perhaps the Birmingham boycott was premier. In fact, Walker played a prominent role in what became the twentieth century's most famous theological protest document:

> The "Letter from a Birmingham Jail" was prompted by local clergymen, a rabbi, and a black minister who said that this was not the time for protest action. Dr. King reacted to it. He was in jail, and his lawyers brought out his comments on the edge of newspapers and toilet paper and whatever paper they could provide him with.
>
> I was the only one in Birmingham who could understand and translate Dr. King's chicken-scratch writing. So I translated it. The Quakers,

or Friends Committee, wanted to call it "Tears of Love," and I told them no. It needed to be called what it was, a letter from a Birmingham jail.

My personal secretary, Willie Pearl Mackey, sat on a typewriter while I translated it, and she typed it. And I remember one night, about 12:30, 1 o'clock, she just was exhausted; she went to sleep on the typewriter, and I moved her over to a chair, and I continued and finished. Because I could type, I finished doing the translation. And then we had to send it back to Dr. King to make sure he was satisfied with it. So it was sent back and forth with his lawyers. So that's the story of the "Letter from a Birmingham Jail," which I think is the most important document of the twentieth century.[27]

My effort to tell the story of our poor people's campaign has benefitted because of my access to Walker, his papers and artifacts, and the *The King of Love* manuscript. The manuscript's draft outline included a prologue and postlogue and eleven chapters. Walker finished the prologue, "The King of Love"; chapter 1, "The Shot Heard Around the World"; and chapter 2, "The First Encounter." He wrote,

As the thirty-second year marking Martin Luther King's brutal assassination passes, this book must be written. With no intention of being grandiose, no one else living can write this book. My dear wife of fifty years has cajoled me for more than a decade to write your King book. At least one hundred and fifty books, at last count, have been published about the life and mission of this towering figure in American affairs of the twentieth century. With rare exception, most have failed to decipher the full mystique of Martin Luther King Jr.[28]

Walker's motivation clearly was to provide an accurate historical record about the mystical King. A thorough reading of his manuscript reveals that Walker had opened a window into his private thoughts and emotions that few, if any, of his other publications have revealed. The following excerpt reveals Walker's loyalty to the legacy of his authentic King, and we take notice of Walker's bold and credible explanation for producing his manuscript:

For all of the above and more, there is a compelling rationale on the basis of this writer's [Walker's] theological connection to King. Both of us are legitimate heirs of the African American free church: both of us are sons of preachers; our God-given intellects were honed by the discipline of completing earned doctorates; our nonviolent credo was fashioned in the classrooms of the academy but also in the trenches of the Egypt-land of the Deep South; both of us have created a credible body of published works; and the center of our being is a personal commitment to Jesus Christ as Savior and Liberator. The uniqueness of these similarities provide an opportunity that so far as I know has not yet been seized by any of our contemporaries of our common struggle.[29]

I have taken necessary time to demonstrate the unique relationship that Walker and King shared from 1951 to 1968. It is "our common struggle" that has obligated us to continue our fight for human rights.

To tell the story of our poor people's campaign, it is clear that we must take advantage of my access to Walker's eyewitness account. In 1964, Walker left the daily operation of the Southern Christian Leadership Conference (SCLC). His reasons are well-known. Dr. Walker and Theresa Ann, his wife, had a young family with basic needs that the SCLC could not provide for. Still, Walker remained intimately close to King. In October 1967, Walker photographed King while both were incarcerated in a Birmingham jail. The iconic photo is synonymous with King's mystique.

King's final days and hours remain controversial and filled with various accounts which have influenced many of us (including me) to be suspicious around the official reports and investigations that followed his death. It is not, however, within my scope here to discuss multiple theories surrounding King's murder. What is important is that Walker has written original material that remains unpublished about those events. Few people have read what follows in the next excerpt:

Ten days earlier, Dr. King had preached the sermon marking my installation as the new pastor of the Canaan Baptist Church of Christ in New York's Harlem community. My wife, Ann, and I left for the West Coast two days later for some rest and relaxation. As fate would have it, our return reservations were fixed for April 4, 1968!

As we entered the front door of our home in Yonkers, a suburb just north of the Bronx, our eldest of three sons, Jay, came bouncing down the stairs and greeted us with the news that *Uncle Martin called last night and said to call him in Memphis.* In the midst of greeting the rest of the siblings and a member of the congregation who had kept house for us a while we were in Los Angeles, Jay came bouncing down the stairs a second time with the ominous report that a television newscast had just been reported that *Uncle Martin's been shot.* I immediately dismissed it as a specious rumor.

Within minutes, [we] were all numbed by the continuing news reports that Martin Luther King Jr., indeed, had been shot and wounded by an unknown assailant in Memphis, Tennessee . . . When I left my house, I still held some irrational hope that the report had to be some kind of cruel hoax.

As I steered my car onto the ramp of the George Washington Bridge, I was listening to New York City's *All News* station, *1010 on your dial.* The car radio seemed to crackle as a newscaster announced *1010, your all-news station now confirms an earlier report that the Reverend Martin Luther King, Jr. has been shot in Memphis, Tennessee—one moment please! Has been shot and killed . . . !* That's where I was when Martin Luther King Jr. was murdered.[30]

Walker admitted that he was stunned by the death of Martin Luther King Jr. His raw emotions are on display and give us rare insight about those in the closest circle around King and how they commonly felt. The next excerpt is lengthy but necessary to help us understand why the continuation of the Poor People's Campaign is the twenty-first-century church's ethical imperative, which is to close the income and wealth gap.

In light of all that had transpired in this sleepy Southern city in the last four hours, one must reflect on the confluence of events that had brought Martin Luther King Jr. to Memphis at this time. It had become a critical detour on the road to the Poor People's Campaign mobilization in which King was immersed. Not many people are aware that the genesis of the Poor People's Campaign had begun in the wake of the Birmingham campaign. Shortly after returning to Atlanta following the historic settlement in the biggest and baddest city in the Deep South, there was considerable optimism within our ranks that if racist Birmingham had capitulated to the forces of nonviolence, no battleground of racial injustice would be inviolate to our assault. In an executive staff meeting at B. B. Beamon's restaurant on Auburn Avenue, Dr. King opined that he was not nearly as sanguine on our optimism. There was no smile on his face as he soberly announced, "Until there is a fairer distribution of wealth in America, we are not going to make any major breakthroughs against racism!" This close-held view was at the heart of the Poor People's Campaign. That and King's stance against the war in Vietnam led to its architect's death.[31]

Walker documented what until now had remained dormant and unknown to many of us. That is, as early as 1963, King and others knew that economic reparations were necessary to make the oppressor and the oppressed legally equal in the public and private institutional spheres. Walker's account provides invaluable insider information into the strategic campaigns that lay at the taproot of the civil rights era's final solution. That is, our final solution is economic reparations, the justification for human rights—the application of our biblical mandate, which the word of reconciliation is.

Indeed, the Poor People's Campaign of 1968 was hindered by the death of Martin Luther King Jr., along with the lack of political support requested and needed from key and pitiful congressional leaders. According to Walker, the Poor People's Campaign was the penultimate climax to the years of toil that ended in a martyr's death. Thus, those who are called to the Du Boisian prophetic tradition believe that our final solution is like Walker's and King's legacy. We are heirs to the struggle for human rights, and therefore we must continue our poor people's campaign. We are contemporary participants in or liberation march, and we are informed by our liberation narrative.

NOTES

1. Wyatt Tee Walker, *The King of Love: My Days with Martin Luther King Jr.* (unpublished manuscript). In 1993, Wyatt Tee Walker began his work on Martin Luther King Jr. but did not finish it. He had given me a copy of the draft and helped me interpret his relationship with Dr. King. In my view, it is his most transparent writing that he produced. I have had a copy of the unfinished manuscript since the summer of 2017. I am told by Dr. Walker's daughter, Patrice Walker Powell, that I am the only person other than his wife,

Mrs. Theresa Ann Walker, to have read the draft. What is significant about the manuscript is that Dr. Walker believed that the Poor People's Campaign is what led to Dr. King's assassination.

2. Ibid. "First Encounters" in *The King of Love: My Days with Martin Luther King, Jr.*, 30.

3. Paul Brockwell Jr., "Let Wyatt Handle This," *University of Richmond Magazine*. https://magazine.richmond.edu/features/article/-/13930/let-wyatt-handle-this.

4. E. Franklin Frazier and C. Eric Lincoln, *The Negro Church in America and The Black Church Since Frazier* (New York: Schocken Books, 1974), 8.

5. Frazier, *Negro Church in America*, 13.

6. Ibid.

7. C. Eric Lincoln, "'Black Power'": A Statement by The Black National Committee of Negro Churchmen," in *The Negro Church in America Since Frazier*, 169.

8. Martin Luther King Jr., "Where Are We Going?", in *Where Do We Go from Here: Chaos or Community?* (Boston: Beacon Press, 1967), 152. King writes about white egoism in this way: "Racism is a tenacious evil, but it is not immutable. Millions of underprivileged whites are in the process of considering the contradiction between segregation and economic progress. *White supremacy can feed their egos but not their stomachs* [italics added]. They will not go hungry or forego the affluent society to remain racially ascendant." For a thorough definition of ethnocentrism see Amos N. Wilson, *Blueprint for Black Power: A Moral, Political, and Economic Imperative for the Twenty-First Century, Essential Readings in the Age of Obama* (New York: Afrikan World InfoSystems, 2014), 102–8. Wilson suggests that if ethnocentrism is carefully considered, it is not necessarily socially evil. However, too often it has been socially evil when employed as an abuse of power: "However, the White Power that has found its way into the central headquarters of the collective Afrikan self-concept is not often felt by Blacks to be alien intrusion into their collective personality because as a part of the self-concept it is perceived to be [a] 'natural' or innate aspect of personality." This is profoundly Du Boisian; it is a redefinition of Du Bois's double consciousness. Wilson continues, "Thus, if Afrikans are to liberate themselves from European domination, empower themselves, enrich their quality of life, they must repudiate the power of Europeans to characterize their ethnicity and through it, gain power over them by characterizing their own perceptions of themselves. Afrikans must become the primary definers of their own ethnicity and determiners of their self-perception, character and behavior. This means that Afrikans must develop a robust, wholesome ethnocentrism. The ethnocentrism of European and Asian nations which exercise global economic and military power is notoriously high. No nation of people can rise to power without pride of nation and race" (108).

9. Henry Louis Gates Jr., *The Signifying Monkey: A Theory of African-American Literary Criticism* (New York: Oxford University Press, 1988).

10. W. E. B. Du Bois, *The Souls of Black Folk* (New York: Bantam Books, 2005), 3.

11. Stokely Carmichael, *Ready for Revolution: The Life and Struggles of Stokely Carmichael [Kwame Ture]* (New York: Simon and Schuster, 2003), 507.

12. Ibid.

13. Wilson, *Blueprint for Black Power*, 89.

14. C. Eric Lincoln, *The Black Church Since Frazier*, 103.

15. Ibid.

16. Ibid., 169.

17. Kenneth Burke, *On Symbols and Society*, ed. Joseph R. Gusfield (Chicago: University of Chicago, 1989), 31. Also see Lucy Hogan and Robert Reid, *Connecting with the Congregation: Rhetoric and the Art of Preaching* (Nashville: Abingdon, 1999), 9–10.

18. Lincoln, "Introduction," 103.

19. Chaim Perelman, *The New Rhetoric: A Treatise on Argumentation*, trans. John Wilkerson and Purcell Weaver (Notre Dame, IN: University of Notre Dame, 1969), 29.

20. Article Three in the Bill of Rights.

21. Ibid.

22. See Cornel West, "Nihilism in Black America," in *Race Matters* (Boston: Beacon Press, 2004), 14–16.

23. Lincoln, *The Black Church Since Frazier*, 169–70.

24. Wilson, *Blueprint for Black Power*, 86.

25. Walker, *King of Love*, 4. The full statement reads, "The primary compelling rationale for this book is the historical connection between Martin Luther King Jr. and the author [Walker]. There is absolutely no substitute for a first-person, eye-witness account."

26. Paul Brockwell Jr., "Let Wyatt Handle This." See: https://magazine.richmond.edu/features/article/-/13930/let-wyatt-handle-this. The article, adapted from an oral history filmed by the University of Richmond film crew was accessed on January 18, 2018.

27. Ibid.

28. Walker, "Prologue," *King of Love*, 4.

29. Ibid., 10.

30. Walker, "The Shot Heard Round the World," *King of Love*, 18–19.

31. Ibid., 28–29.

CHAPTER
3

Our Pan-African Liberation Narrative and Its Globalized Influence

One of the key lessons learnt from the history of liberation theology is the centrality of contextuality, the significance of "where one stands" when thinking about and discussing these matters. This is not only true of the history of theology for as long as we can remember; it is also true for the Bible, both for the way in which biblical narratives are being told and for the way in which those narratives are being read, understood, interpreted and retold. The context of telling is as important as the context of retelling. Hence it is vital to hold onto the significance and meaning of this important sentence.[1] –Allan Boesak

All human narratives emerge from sociopolitical, economic, and moral contexts. For oppressed people, our narrative's emergence is aligned predominately with our liberation march, which personifies our dogged pursuit for equality through human rights (i.e., reconciliation through economic restitution). In the previous chapter, an attempt was made to affirm this plausible argument; that is, our liberation march and narrative were born of crisis. Second, our liberation narrative continues to evolve alongside radical sociopolitical, economic, and moral changes in our global culture. Thus, we are able to trace our liberation narrative's evolution from a Negro pathology toward a pan-African ideology. Third, in this chapter we make an additional claim, which is that the black narrative has continued to evolve into what is called here a pan-African liberation narrative. Fourth, readers will see later, we claim that our pan-African liberation march and narrative is the way forward for all oppressed people globally. Finally, we make an attempt to reinforce these claims in the multiracial Dutch Reformed Church's Accra Confession (2004).

From the beginning, I have referred to black folks as people of African descent, and for this reason: to foreshadow these social changes and to avoid limitations that may cause a too-narrow focus not appropriate for our liberation march and narrative. Instead, our liberation march and narrative is collectively shared in a global context. In short, wherever people of African descent experience Eurocentric hegemonic practices, a similar liberation march and narrative is common among the oppressed, namely, people of African descent. As indicated, however, we now see traces of our liberation motifs in the aspirations of multiple races of oppressed people globally.

Shared common experiences among any people group make it plausible that a sociopsychological, hermeneutic, and narrative collectivism functions and furthermore shapes human cultural identities (i.e., political, economic, cultural, hermeneutic, narrative, rhetoric, theology, and homiletic). If this is plausible, it is reasonable to suggest that people of African descent and specifically in the United States have become recognized globally as the twenty-first century's heroic figures because we have survived racists' inhuman indecencies despite the efforts of the world's greatest empire, the United States. These indecencies include genocidal slavery, eugenics-like Jim and Jane Crow lynching, poll taxes, segregation, unfair and inadequate housing, unaffordable healthcare, unemployment, underemployment, undereducation, and overincarceration. In short, we possess a powerfully cathartic, redemptive, and reconciling story that now demands socioeconomic equalities through human rights efforts such as restorative economic justice.

The narrative of people of African descent in America is a species of rhetoric, and in this instance, a trope and metaphor which, readers will see later, undergirds the twenty-first century's emergent pan-African liberation narrative. The narrative of people of African descent is also political. Indeed, it exposes the flaw lines of the culturally dominating Eurocentric narrative. Suffering that people of African descent have endured, and continue to endure, are traceable to past, present, and foreseeable Eurocentric classes, culture, and pathology. We locate our suffering in the Eurocentric narrative. I posit that this narrative is biased factually and therefore oftentimes is unbalanced and untruthful. If a sociohistorical narrative is biased politically and otherwise, the narrative becomes undemocratic, exclusive, and hegemonic. These biases may skew biblical exegesis. To avoid this error, we contend that another narrative which has been nearly invisible to dominating classes and culture has surfaced already. That narrative is the pan-African liberation narrative.

The Emergent Pan-African Liberation Narrative

We now turn toward Allan Boesak, a scholar and theologian from South Africa, to develop further our liberation narrative, called here the pan-African liberation narrative. Boesak is an heir of the Du Boisian prophetic tradition. His ideas and commitment to liberation have been compared with those of Karl Marx.[2] Of course Marx was not a religionist, as is Boesak. I avoid labels such as Marxist or Marxism, because these labels are Eurocentric constructs and considered blasphemous to advocates of so-called market-driven forms of capitalism. It is not germane to our objectives whether Boesak is Marxist or capitalist. What is germane is that Boesak is Du Boisian and a proponent of our pan-African liberation narrative. Boesak's liberation ideology is consistent with biblical Old and New Testament motifs (e.g., Exodus 12:33-36; Mark 10:17-31). These and other similar biblical texts informed the Du Boisian prophetic tradition and how we understand that God is a liberator and the true and living God who demands reconciliatory justice and restitution.

By locating Boesak in our liberation context, we see that he is engaged in our constant and common struggle to achieve human rights in the face of oppressive systems. For Boesak, the contours of his liberation march and narrative began to form on the banks of the Orange River near Kakamas, a South African village. Liberation motifs are born of crisis, and this was the case for Boesak. His father, Willie, who was an educator, died in 1953, forcing his mother, Sarah, and his siblings to move to Boland, which resulted in a lower standard of living. There, Sarah became a laborer, which forced the Boesak family to experience abject poverty in a dysfunctional society reinforced by unfettered socio-political and economic racism. This system is known broadly as apartheid. It was this oppressive regime, apartheid, that radicalized Boesak.[3]

Apartheid came to international attention in the 1980s. It began through colonial rule, and we can point directly toward the occupation by the Netherlands and the British Empire. Since the mid-1700s these two colonial powers ruled what is now called South Africa. In 1834, the British government abolished slavery; the regime of human inequality, however, continued. The official establishment of South African minority home rule began in 1948. The following excerpt summarizes the history of white South African oppression over indigenous blacks:

> By 1940, the white minority regime had consolidated its power and had established a racially segregated society in which the white settlers had absolute domination of landownership, the legal system, the political process, the distribution of wealth, and control of every phase of social relationships. Industrialization had produced a black urban working class which became increasingly militant and restive under minority rule.[4]

Apartheid was an antagonist for people of African descent and nothing short of racist terrorism. This regime birthed South Africa's liberation march and narrative that we claim people of African descent share globally. This human crisis induced the birth of resistance to empire and a counternarrative, that is, our liberation march and narrative. But the liberation narrative and, in this case, the pan-African liberation narrative, is also a protagonist and catalyst, another informant for those called to the Du Boisian prophetic tradition.

What follows is an example of how this claim is noticed in the evolution of Boesak's moral consciousness. We shall see that politics and theology inform Boesak's worldview and impel him front and center where he discovers himself in the middle of our liberation march and narrative. Thus we shall see the role that social context plays. Boesak's biographer identifies that Boesak's moment of crisis was apartheid, which can only be described as a systemic oppressive and racist regime:

The theme continually recurring throughout Allan Boesak's numerous books, addresses and sermons is his intense resistance to apartheid. His opinions can be grouped roughly into categories: the political and the theological. The first group deserves our initial attention and it is from this that his theological opinions are largely derived. By analyzing his attitude of mind we can form a better understanding of his actions.[5]

As indicated, Boesak is an heir of the Du Boisian prophetic tradition, in part because Boesak understands the nexus that exists between political and theological constructs. These are inseparable. Too often, these constructs are used as means to oppress and segregate people for economic advantages. Our understanding of Boesak's radicalization is largely aided by this: Politics must have a moral underpinning. Liberation theology must have a political underpinning. Both are informed by social realities that occur in particular places and times.

What has become clear is that we must respond to global crises by forming a new global politics, which demands a new global theology and narrative. For this to be accepted, all oppressed people must enlist in our liberation march—the march of Du Bois, King, Walker, Carmichael, and Boesak. Before people of African descent and other people who are oppressed can employ our liberation march and narrative, they must believe it. This will require a new consciousness. Our next step is to embrace our collective new consciousness.

A Pan-African Narrative and Our New Consciousness

Since the 1970s, Allan Boesak has been at the forefront of our liberation march and narrative. Liberation theology and other aspects of the ideology, according to Boesak, are informed by a new consciousness:

We cannot understand liberation theology, whether in South Africa, in Latin America, or other parts of the Third World [and the United States and other locations where people of African descent are located], unless we understand that it developed within a framework of a new political consciousness. People became aware, first of all, of their own situations. There was a new consciousness of themselves, of where they were, of the political, social and economic dynamics in their situations. When people began to understand their situations, they started asking questions they had never asked before. . . .

The first question that we ask when we get this new consciousness is WHY? In asking "WHY?" we begin to discover that we have lived through a theological tradition [informed through Eurocentrism and its lens] that, although it was our own, was really never our own. It has always been controlled by people who also control the political parties, the economic and social situation, our very lives. In South Africa we have a particular situation that we call "apartheid." Apartheid is not only a political system; it is not only an economic and social system. It is also a theological reality. Perhaps the distinction of color is stressed, but just the same "apartheid" is a religion, just as all forms of racism become religions.[6]

New consciousness is not a new concept, nor is it exclusive to Boesak. Stokely Carmichael, a pan-African leader best known for popularizing the slogan "Black Power," defined (new) consciousness and its necessity in this way:

Consciousness more than anything else is what separates humanity from other animals. Consciousness is attained by the acquisition of knowledge. This is a continual process in a conscious life. All conscious people, and especially we Africans, have the responsibility to struggle through a barrage of information and misinformation . . . so as to properly understand the social, political and economic conflicts that affect us. Thus to understand our historical duty [is] to advance the transformation of our people and societies to a better, more humane way of life. This is a lifelong responsibility. It begins with [new] consciousness.[7]

Boesak and Carmichael are a part of the Du Boisian prophetic tradition in this sense: both are aware that our new consciousness reinforces our liberation narrative. What is of import here, whether we emphasize a new consciousness or a new narrative, is that these evolve from the immediate sociopolitical, economic, and racial crises which point toward our situational context.

A new consciousness makes people aware of their own agency to cause change. A new consciousness inspires a sense of self-determined identity and self-worth, an understanding that power is necessary to overcome powerlessness. Power or new consciousness is "a call for Afrikan Americans to critically examine the origins and functions of the rules, morals, values, customary attitudes and behavior, common perspectives and folkways they [people of African descent] have been convinced to accept as the result of White American physical and coercive impositions, ideological propaganda and continuing procedures."[8]

A new consciousness is a new power that informs our liberation march and narrative, born of crisis. It creates a new situational context and environment to resist conformity to Eurocentric norms such as the Eurocentric narrative. Boesak then rightly understands that a new consciousness is necessary to embrace liberation motifs, which are necessary to advance our equalities through our human rights agenda. A new consciousness for Du Boisan thinkers must be grasped in order to fulfill our calling. Our calling is to seek human transformation through the means of the word of reconciliation and justified restitution.

Our liberation march and narrative is reinforced by our new consciousness and is our point of departure and how we understand and apply the word of reconciliation. As you will see in later chapters, there are Old and New Testament passages that define reconciliation as "change or exchange." For now, we define the word of reconciliation as a means for closing the income and wealth inequality gap. To do so, and among other things, we must contend with overcoming inadequate education, healthcare, technological disadvantages, government regimes, and generational income and wealth distributions that continue to draw interest. Through careful estate planning, these economic windfalls are passed on to ensuing generations. Pan-Africanist scholar Amos N. Wilson makes this clear:

> Consequently, while prior forms of White domination and exploitation of Blacks may have ceased and desisted, the economic injustices and inequalities they imposed continue unabated. The legal prohibition of further injustices does not necessarily mean that the injurious effects of past injustices no longer persist and do not require rectification.

Justice requires not only the ceasing and desisting of injustice but also requires punishment or reparation for injuries and damages inflicted for prior wrongdoing. The essence of injustice is the redistribution of gains earned through the perpetuation of injustice. If restitution is not made and reparations not instituted to compensate for prior injustices, those injustices are in effect rewarded.[9]

We can summarize Wilson's remarks as something similar to a moral and legal claim that an attorney may present before a judicial bar.[10] Wilson opens the door to a discussion about what restitution looks like in our litigious culture. His focus here is on forms of domination and exploitation of people of African descent and that such exploitation continues unabated despite changes in federal, state, and municipal laws. What remains is cultural privilege to race and the dominating classes. What continues is economic injustice, which requires, if not demands, redistribution of income and wealth. Our remedy points squarely toward economic reparations.

There are two species of legal and binding economic justice. The first is retributive; the second is restorative. Retributive justice views economic injustices as crime in terms of illegal acts against a certain state. The state holds an offender or offenders accountable and a court of law defines what binds punitive actions and a means to reconcile differences between the offenders and the offended. Restorative justice, by contrast, views injustices as crime in terms of being acts against a person, persons, or a community. This may be understood as a class-action suit against the state or another party or parties held accountable, and the state or party is made to take responsibility for providing legal and binding remedies to repair the aggrieved and their community at large.[11]

Restorative justice focuses on priestly healing and the prophetic future. In this way, people of African descent and other oppressed people will benefit from economic reparations and structural changes to the system or systems that have caused historical injuries. This species of justice holds accountable the state, which in the case of African Americans has sanctioned, since the founding of the American republic, rights to enslave, purchase, and trade human bodies on the open market. The psychological damage continued long after 1865. We keep in mind here that people of African descent in America did not have our guaranteed legal right to vote until 1965. Between 1865 and 1965 we have endured and survived separate-but-equal, Jim and Jane Crow, the poll tax, human lynching, and numerous disadvantages that have led us to this point where we must demand legal and binding economic justice, which is our human right.

Lennox Hinds, author of "Apartheid in South Africa and the Universal Declaration of Human Rights," argues that human rights for people of African descent would not have been recognized legally in the South African courts alone. Instead, these rights came due in part to a universal declaration against apartheid. In short, minority rule in South Africa was not compelled to grant equal citizenship under their laws. In Paris, France, three years after the Allied defeat of fascism, the United Nations ratified a document called the Universal Document of Human Rights (1948). During that time, George Marshall was the US Secretary of State. His reasons for supporting the declaration are as follows:

> Systematic and deliberate denials of basic human rights lie at the root of most of our troubles and threaten the work of the United Nations. It is not only fundamentally wrong that millions of men and women live in daily terror of secret police, subject to seizure, imprisonment, or forced labor without just cause and without fair trial, but these wrongs have repercussions in the community of nations. Governments which systematically disregard the rights of their own people are not likely to respect the rights of other nations and other people and are likely to seek their objectives by coercion and force in the international field.[12]

If Marshall is to be taken literally, he has described South Africa as a police state, not as a democracy. He points to state-sanctioned terrorism and a total disregard of all citizens' civil rights. What is more, Marshall suggests that South African apartheid gave indication that the world of nations may be subject to international coercion, which was considered to be a threat to democracy everywhere.

This brief historical summary of apartheid terrorism is indispensable to the plausibility of our argument. The General Assembly of the United Nations's intervention in 1948 is our essential framework. The Universal Document for Human Rights is a point of departure for the Accra Confession (2004). However, our pan-African liberation narrative influenced the confession's content.

The Pan-African Liberation Narrative and
Its Influence on the Accra Confession

Our task here is to bring several ideas together into a persuasive consensus. As previously stated, significant to our argument is the Universal Declaration of Human Rights. We see two ironies associated with the declaration. First, it condemns inhumanly abusive acts sanctioned by the South African regime against its citizens of African descent. Second, the declaration's condemnations of South African pathology warn that its pathology is similar to that of an emerging empire. In short, the Accra Confession argues that the emerging empire threatens the sovereignty of states in the world.

Another part of our task then is to provide plausibility that the Accra Confession is largely influenced by pan-African liberation motifs and particularly liberation motifs commonly held by the Global South (formerly called Third-World nations). It is the Global South that has warned consistently of empire; it and other African countries have experienced colonialism and so-called postcolonialism.[13] Empire, however, is created by people, but empire controls the very people who have created it. The empire that the Accra Confession addresses is similar to the apocalyptic fourth beast that is described in the books of Daniel and Revelation (Daniel 7:7-8; Revelation 13). The fourth beast is an amalgamation of the previous beasts or empires. This fourth beast that Daniel envisioned and John saw is an unrivaled empire that has consolidated all of the previous empires' power.

The Accra Confession caused tension among affiliated churches. Out of crisis, and inspired by the challenge that is inherent in the confession, German and African churches, a part of the Globalization Project, provided the following definition of empire:

> We speak of empire, because we discern a coming together of economic, cultural, political and military power in our world today. This is constituted by a reality and a spirit of lordless domination, created by humankind. An all-encompassing global reality serving, protecting and defending the interest of powerful corporations, nations, elites and privileged people, while exploiting creation, imperiously excludes, enslaves and even sacrifices humanity. It is a perverse spirit of destructive

self-interest, even greed—the worship of money, goods and possessions; the gospel of consumerism, proclaimed through powerful propaganda and religiously justified, believed and followed. It is colonization of consciousness, values and notions of human life by the imperial logic; a spirit of lacking compassionate justice and showing contemptuous disregard for the gifts of creation and the household of life.[14]

Because of the empire's invincibility, there is a need for prophetic language that envisions a hopeful future. As Boesak explains, this is "the language that the worldwide family of Reformed churches has spoken in the Accra Confession adopted in 2004, which deals with the reality of empire, economic and social justice, the destruction of the earth, the threat to God's vulnerable children, and the response of faith."[15] Boesak claims that the Accra Confession is a document that focuses on empire, and in the face of empire, the confession is a bold challenge for us to reconsider the word of reconciliation in a global context.

Boesak is widely recognized as an abolitionist against South African apartheid. Before this, however, Boesak has been a contributor to our pan-African liberation narrative which I have asserted influenced the content of the Accra Confession. A significant point of departure for liberation theology and our narrative is that each is organic to the socio-political and economic conditions that are associated with that current context. By this, I mean social location shapes the human narrative.

The Accra Confession, adopted by the World Alliance of Reformed Churches (WARC), was a response to an undeniably visible global empire, namely, the United States of America. Boesak characterizes the confession's context and then comments on its meaning:

"Discerning the signs of the times" is the framework within which the General Council of the World Alliance of Reformed Churches (WARC) has chosen to set its deliberations, out of which flowed "The Accra Confession" (2004). The times we live in, the document argues, are times of great urgency, global economic injustice and ecological destruction. The times depict a "scandalous world" of harsh, utterly shocking and growing inequalities across the world among and within nations, resource-driven wars, poverty and disease, of which the most vulnerable victims are women and children. These are time of wanton, profit-driven destruction of the earth and rapacious plundering of her resources, which all are part of "a crisis directly related to the development of neo-liberal economic globalization" (The Accra Confession 2004: para. 9).[16]

What we are facing is "coming together," a coalescing of global forces, pooling their resources and power—of economic, political, cultural, and military. It is no longer the marshalling of national assets, arsenals, and governmental powers in "defense of democracy," for "the protection of civilization" in an imagined "clash of civilizations," in the name of the "war on terror."

The empire we face is created by humankind; it is not divinely sanctioned, God-given, or historically determined; it is not irreversible, unchangeable, as it is claimed. The language we use—in the way we speak of "the Markets," for example—sets up the deification of the markets as a normal thing, as if they were godlike entities that determine, in and of themselves, the destiny of individuals and nations, masking the truth that "the markets" are in fact determined by the rules set up and manipulated by those who control the global capitalist system. It does another thing: it masks the persistent violence inherent in that manipulation, the destruction it wreaks on whole communities for the sake of profits for the few. There is nothing godlike about it. We are called instead to discern the anti-godlike spirit that drives reality. And because it is anti-God, it is antihuman.[17]

Boesak's prophetic liberation motifs are informed by pan-Africanism. Boesak, like Du Bois, synthesizes and characterizes empire in this way: Boesak focuses on abusive military and political power and the consolidation of corporations' economic resources, sanctioned by undifferentiating and permissive government regimes. The largest and most alarming claim that Boesak makes is that the empire's "market" is the beast.

The Accra Confession affirms that economic globalization is reinforced by neo-liberalism's two-headed beast, which is an overwhelming presence of political and military superiority. The United States, through neo-liberalism, then, imposes its will over sovereign countries' governments and markets. Its justification is that empire is superior to lesser nations' traditions, mores, values, cultures, myths, and religions. To describe neo-liberalism as empire and economic globalization as world domination, the following words appear in the confession: "unrestrained competition, consumerism, unlimited economic growth and accumulation of wealth . . . unrestricted access for foreign investments and imports . . . unrestricted movement of capital."[18] Furthermore, the confession posits that advocates of neoliberalism make the false claim that "[empire] will achieve wealth for all;" and that "social obligations, protection of the poor and weak, trade unions, and relationships between people are subordinate to the processes of economic growth and capital accumulation."[19]

In short, the writers of the confession describe capitalism and how it is used to justify the presence of empire and its supremacist tentacles that strangle the weak and suffocate the disinherited. Capitalism is anti-human. It cannot feel the struggling masses. It does not care about the needs of the poor and oppressed. By definition, those who have created the beast are agnostics and nihilistic. By its greed, lust, envy, jealousy, and hatred, the beast is driven and controls its idolatrous disciples.

It is significant to note that like the World Council of Reformed Churches, which met in Accra, Ghana, in 2004, the pan-African Conference of Third World Theologians met there in December 1977. What do these different theological conclaves have in common? Although their conferences occurred nearly three decades apart, both groups found it necessary to claim and refine their liberation march and narrative. I contend that this African invention (liberation march and narrative) is akin to the Du Boisian prophetic tradition, our informant to our liberation march and narrative. That is, both are born of a critical survival struggle, which by definition is our attempt to resist empire's suffocating grip and grasp. According to Boesak, the author of *Liberation Theology in South Africa*, we can resist suffocation by embracing our emergent new consciousness that encourages us, if not forces us, to develop our pan-African liberation narrative.

The lived experiences of the oppressed are dogged. Historically we have been subjugated to a closed economic and political system that is segregated, which is another expression of Boesak's apartheid. This condition is global, reinforced by Eurocentrism and its Eurocentric narrative, the catalyst of neo-liberalism. Therefore, a different narrative must emerge, a narrative that we have come to know as a pan-African liberation narrative.

Conclusion

In short, the pan-African liberation narrative must serve as a corrective that replaces the Eurocentric narrative. Our liberation narrative inspires Du Bosian preachers and thinkers with a megaphone to sound the global alarm. The alarm is similar to our new consciousness, which is necessary in order to confront the dominating cultures' and classes' antagonistic narrative. Thus, the pan-African liberation narrative must be defined as a new consciousness, an independent pathology that is shaped by the existential, reflective, and collective experiences of oppressed people, namely, people of African descent. We have made a plausible argument that pan-Africanism and the pan-African liberation march and narrative serve as the model for all oppressed people, people of African descent and otherwise who make an attempt to march as faithful and authentic Christians, people who doggedly pursue the God of liberation, reconciling justice and equality, which is nothing less than the word of reconciliation.

We have expressed our liberation march and narrative as a weapon to confront the racist, oppressive regime known as apartheid. "Apartheid is not only a political system; it is not only an economic and social system. It is also a theological reality . . . apartheid is a religion, just as all forms of racism become religions."[20] Apartheid then is the continuation of colonial and postcolonial power and occupation. We must remember that apartheid was ended by international political and theological pressures: the General Assembly of the United Nations and the pan-African theologians, particularly those located in the Global South and the Dutch Reformed Church and its Accra Confession.

Furthermore, we have made an attempt to demonstrate that apartheid was the foreshadow of the emergent empire which was expressed first in General Assembly of the United Nation's Universal Declaration of Human Rights and secondly in The Declaration and the Pan-African Conference of Third World Theologians that convened in Accra, Ghana (1977). These declarations are our point of departure to emphasize the historic significance of the Accra Confession (2004). The Accra Confession plainly states that American neo-liberalism's two-headed beast—namely, military and political power—is a threat to the world of nations. Neo-liberalism is a servant of empire, and in this way it imposes its will upon other sovereign countries, influencing global markets. It is nothing less than the apocalyptic beast of Daniel and the Revelator (Daniel 7:7-8; Revelation 13).

We have defined our liberation march and narrative as our pursuit of human rights through economic justice. Restorative justice is an approach that leads to economic reparations for people of African descent. Finally, in this chapter, we have sought to make a plausible argument that our liberation march and narrative is a global movement and message, and in this instance we have made known that it has lifted the veil over empire. Empire's market-driven goals and objectives are sinister and inspire a racialized culture that controls the masses. I gravely believe that empire's market-driven culture is an antihuman, lordless religion, and it is toward a biblical antidote to that lordless religion that we shall turn in the next two chapters.

Chapters four and five, "The Word of Reconciliation Reconsidered: Matthew 5–7, 2 Corinthians 5:16-20, and Creating a New Consciousness" and "Passover, Our Collective Liberation Narrative: Exodus 12, Luke 19:1-10, and Shaping a Claim for Justice," are an attempt to delve underneath lordless religion. Indeed, our toxicity is located in the aforementioned and current racialized culture that indeed controls the masses' impulses which crave instant gratification. Of course, this implies that many of us are unaware of Old and New Testament texts which persuade us to embrace a new consciousness. It is the new consciousness that lifts the veil over Eurocentrism's tentacles of greed that tightly grab hold of us and by way of market-driven economies we are enslaved to them. Therefore, it is imperative that we find biblical reconciliation, reconciliation that supports my claim that income and wealth inequalities have and continue to exist. It is my intention in these next two chapters to confront and surgically remove lordless religion, religion that possesses toxic power but power that can be recognized and treated by spiritual antidotes and when necessary with spiritual surgery. The radicalized preacher's scalpel is prophetic preaching supported by radicalized Scriptures.

NOTES

1. Allan Boesak, "Theological Reflections on Empire," *HTS Teologiese Studies / Theological Studies* 65 (2009), no. 1, Art. #291. DOI: https:/doi.org/10.4102/hts.v65i1.291, 646.

2. Albert Scholtz, *The Story of Allan Boesak* (Germany: Busse-Seewald, 1989), 7.

3. Ibid., 10.

4. Lennox S. Hinds, "Apartheid in South Africa and the Universal Declaration of Human Rights," *Crime and Social Justice* 24 (1985): 5–43.

5. Scholtz, *Story of Allan Boesak*, 22.

6. Allan Boesak, "Liberation Theology in South Africa," in *African Theology en Route: Papers from the Pan African Conference of Third World Theologians, December 17–23, 1977, Accra, Ghana*, ed. Kofi Appiah-Kubi and Sergio Torres (Maryknoll, NY: Orbis, 1979), 169.

7. Stokely Carmichael, *Ready for Revolution: The Life and Struggles of Stokely Carmichael* (New York: Scribner, 2003), 674.

8. Amos N. Wilson, *Blueprint for Black Power: A Moral, Political, and Economic Imperative for the Twenty-First Century*, 8th ed. (New York: Afrikan World InfoSystems, 2017), 20.

9. Ibid., 459.

10. See Rhonda E. Howard-Hassmann and Anthony P. Lombardo, "Framing Reparations Claims: Differences between the African and Jewish Social Movements for Reparations," *African Studies Review* vol. 50, no. 1 (April 2007): 27–48. "Moreover, the principal actor promoting discussion of historical reparations as a new norm of justice was the United Nations High Commission for Human Rights, which organized the Durban Conference that addressed global reparations for people of African descent and people of color" (30).

11. http://www.cscsb.org/restorative_justice/retribution_vs_restoration.html, accessed March 18, 2017.

12. Hinds, "Apartheid in South Africa," 6.

13. In a personal interview conducted on March 13, 2017, Boesak made this statement in response to my questions about the influence pan-Africanism had on the Accra Confession: "The World Alliance of Reformed Churches is an ecumenical body. Yes, it has Eurocentric beginnings, but in the 1980s it was strongly influenced by theological and political thinking from the Global South. The Apartheid Is a Heresy Declaration, followed by the Accra Confession (there is a logical theological continuation) and the subsequent debates on neo-liberal capitalist, consumerist, ecocidal ideologies and practices and their impact on the dignity of human life and the integrity of creation as heresy— these are all the consequences of the influence of Global South (and particu-

larly pan-African) perspectives. Both the Apartheid Declaration and the Accra Confession began as initiatives of Africans. In short, yes, the Accra document has strong characteristics of a pan-Africanist document."

14. Allan Aubrey Boesak, *Dare We Speak of Hope? Searching for a Language of Life in Faith and Politics* (Grand Rapids: Eerdmans, 2014), 56.

15. Ibid., 51.

16. Boesak, "Theological Reflections on Empire," 645.

17. In a personal interview conducted on March 13, 2017, I asked Boesak, "[Are you] a pan-Africanist and which publication that you've written best describes your pan-Africanism?" Boesak said, "I do consider myself a pan-Africanist but have not worked on that explicit label. I do associate myself strongly with the work of Mahmood Mamdani (see the chapter on Ubuntu in my forthcoming publication) and my current work (on a revisitation of some aspects of black liberation theology) is a strong engagement with pan-Africanist (feminist) theological thought. The African women engaged in critical theological, postcolonial, anti-imperial work prefer to call themselves African feminists rather than womanist, which as you know is a very particularly African American term."

18. The Accra Confession, para. 9. www.wcrc.ch/accra/the-accra-confession.

19. Ibid.

20. Allan Boesak, "Liberation Theology in South Africa" in *African Theology in Route* eds. Kofi Appiah Kubi and Sergio Torres (Marynoll, NY: Orbis Books, 1979), 169.

PART 2

Preaching for Economic Justice

CHAPTER 4.

The Word of Reconciliation Reconsidered

Matthew 5–7, 2 Corinthians 5:16-20, and Creating a New Consciousness

In a sense we've come to our nation's capital to cash a check. When the architects of our republic wrote the magnificent words of the Constitution and the Declaration of Independence, they were signing a promissory note to which every American was to fall heir. This note was the promise that all men, yes, black men as well as white men, would be guaranteed the unalienable rights of life, liberty, and the pursuit of happiness.

It is obvious today that America has defaulted on this promissory note in so far as her citizens of color are concerned. Instead of honoring this sacred obligation, America has given the Negro people a bad check, a check; which has come back marked "insufficient funds."[1] —Martin Luther King Jr., "I Have a Dream"

August 28, 1963, the temperature in Washington, DC, was 83 degrees with a dew point beneath 50 percent.[2] Because of the record numbers of people gathered to hear Dr. Martin Luther King Jr. speak on the nation's mall was overcrowded, with an estimated 250,000 people, the heat index seemed to be higher. Others listened and watched around the world. Standing on the steps of the Lincoln Memorial, King witnessed a sea of faces aligned on both sides of the reflecting pool. In the distance, he looked at one of America's most recognizable symbols of democracy and empire, the dome of the nation's Capital.

King wore his traditional black suit, white shirt, black tie, and black shoes. At the appropriate time, he delivered his ionic message, "I Have a Dream." King's message was approximately seventeen minutes in length. Because of the occasion, content, delivery, and historical significance, his oratory is described as one of the most significant public addresses of the twentieth century. Our opening epithet is a part of King's oratorical thesis. It is here, however, that we present the continuing part of his thesis:

> We refuse to believe that there are insufficient funds in the great vaults of opportunity of this nation. And so we've come to cash this check, a check that will give us upon demand the riches of freedom and the security of justice.[3]

King's oratory is a civic sermon.[4] What then was King's objective? Did he intentionally seek to create a new consciousness? Did King introduce a cultural paradigm shift?[5] Did King communicate to the dominating culture that its barons continued (and continue) to benefit disproportionately through an unethical financial infrastructure? Did King's audience understand that he was prophesying against the nation's immoral but legalized practices that were crafted as legislation, presented as policies to protect the elite?

Did King use his civic sermon to emphasize that white Americans had become deceived and comfortable with a Greco-Roman mythology, which is the aesthetic origin and invention of white privilege? This privilege has blinded majorities of blacks and whites and permitted many to believe that people of African descent are predestined to remain members of an unjust caste system in perpetuity.

In order to reconcile these age-old sins of hegemonic bigotry and racism, King communicated that it had become long overdue that a new consciousness and cultural paradigm shift be birthed. King did use this context, setting, and rhetorical situation to present a reconsideration of what the word of reconciliation means. Indeed, such a word is necessary to achieve economic restitution.

As mentioned in the book's second chapter, King made it clear that economic restitution was the penultimate objective of the civil rights movement.[6] It is clear that King understood that his words mattered. King's rhetoric placed America's sociomarginalized and segregated people of African descent at the edge of our Americanized Jordan River. By leading legions to the river's edge, King signaled to the dominating classes what had been signaled to people of African descent since the Harlem Renaissance: the birth of a new cultural consciousness. This consciousness came with a paradigm shift that demanded human equality, justice, and economic reparations. This is the protagonist's insurgency that continues to evolve in the Eurocentric psyche among dominating classes and the sociomarginalized. We see its influence in persons such as Howard Schultz, the CEO of Starbucks, and his philanthropic philosophy. Schultz preaches giving and philanthropy; his company financially reinvests into the coffee farms of people groups of African descent.[7]

King's new paradigm re-presented the "word of reconciliation" by persuading people like Schultz that its meaning goes beyond the obvious, which are its salvific implications. King expanded the word of reconciliation to also mean human justice. Reconciliation is understood to be the fulfillment of justice. This justice requires democratic demands that include economic reparations. King's civil rights campaign was successful in part because he was able to change the debate, a debate that was accepted reluctantly in the dominating culture's public and private spheres. It was at this time King understood that the civil rights movement had been globalized, as Lewis Baldwin describes: "[King's] vision gradually transcended Southern particularism to assume national and international implications."[8] What is necessary here is to note that King's paradigm shift has informed our contemporary cultural worldview to see that reconciliation is a human justice motif, which is a biblical mandate.

Reconciliation as a Human Justice Motif

Justice then is related directly to reconciliation. By following the narrative in the Gospel of Matthew, we notice the emerging justice motif. In Matthew 4:23-25, we see and hear crowds who followed Jesus throughout Galilee. In Capernaum of Galilee, Jesus proclaims the gospel of the kingdom. He proclaims, teaches, and heals. A prominent feature of the

Gospel of Matthew is that Jesus exorcised the demonic presence from the possessed:

> Jesus went throughout Galilee, teaching in their synagogues, proclaiming the good news of the kingdom, and healing every disease and sickness among the people. News about him spread all over Syria, and people brought to him all who were ill with various diseases, those suffering severe pain, the demon-possessed, those having seizures, and the paralyzed; and he healed them. Large crowds from Galilee, the Decapolis, Jerusalem, Judea and the region across the Jordan followed him. (Matthew 4:23-25, NIV)

In this way, we can visualize and understand why the crowds followed Jesus. But these verses mean more. They serve to segue to the Sermon on the Mount and set into context the socioeconomic and psychospiritual location of Jesus' new followers. Most were destitute and desperate. In short, the sociomarginalized people were demonized by dominating empire. Jesus came to exorcise the demonic power of empire by diminishing its presence in the lives of the people of Galilee of Capernaum. This is the central focus of the Sermon on the Mount.

The Gospel of Matthew (chapters 5–7) records the Sermon on the Mount. Jesus' discourse begins with the Beatitudes (5:1-12). He then teaches about Ethical Disciples in an Unethical World (5:13-20); Personal Behavior and Community Relationships (5:21-48); Corporate and Individual Giving to Sociomarginalized People and Corporate Prayer (6:1-14); Fasting as a Weapon Against Materialism (6:16-24); How Believers Process Anxieties (6:25-34); How to Identify Biases (7:1-6); An Ethical Prayer (7:7-12); Righteous Judgment (7:15-23); and Making Ethical Choices and Consequences (7:24-29).[9]

An incisive reader of Matthew's Gospel will discover that Jesus' focus is not only on the obvious demonic presence and power of empire; instead, the reader will grasp that Jesus creates a new consciousness, a new cultural paradigm. To the oppressed, Jesus introduces the principles of the kingdom of God in the human realm. God's kingdom principles are counterintuitive to hegemonic power; those principles describe an alternative reality that is realized by faith, and that faith, in the future, has come into our sights, sounds, smells, and zip codes.

God's kingdom principles make Jesus' disciples independent of empire. Thus independence from empire's values and beliefs liberated oppressed people and made us accountable to make ethical decisions congruent with the kingdom of God: "Now when Jesus had finished saying these things, the crowds were astounded at his teaching, for he taught them as one having authority, and not as their scribes" (Matthew 7:28-29, NRSV). In fact, Jesus taught that reconciliation must first take place within our community. In other words, Jesus has taken steps to create a new consciousness in order to form a new cultural paradigm to shape and form our new community. We have been given a glimpse of the emerging kingdom of God. We sense its presence, its traits, and its characteristics in the human realm.

A closer reading of Matthew 5:21-30 indicates that Jesus focused his audience's attention on personal behavior and community relationships. In short, Jesus talked about what we can control, not about what we cannot control. "So when you are offering your gift at the altar, if you remember that your brother or sister has something against you, leave your gift there before the altar and go; first be reconciled to your brother or sister, and then come and offer your gift" (Matthew 5:23-24, NRSV).

The larger context (Matthew 5:21-30) further indicates that informed by God's kingdom principles, Jesus wants his oppressed audience to find ways to resolve their differences within the kingdom of God and not inside empire's courts. Expressed another way, the oppressed are charged with resolving our differences in an ecclesial court system, something that is personal. In a few words, Christian believers become our own court, jury, and judge—we are called to solve our differences among ourselves.

Of course, the Sermon on the Mount is difficult to interpret exactly. We do know that Jesus employs hyperbole and metaphoric language with indigenous preunderstandings and connotations. What is certain is that Jesus focuses on humanity's role in personal and community reconciliation. Did King do the same? That is, did he focus his audience's attention around his interpretation of Jesus' ethic? Did King reframe Jesus' rhetorical situation and make it into his own? Did King speak to the people aligned along the reflecting pool in the same way that Jesus spoke atop that mountain near the Sea of Galilee?

I think so. It is plausible and useful to believe that King's "I Have a Dream" is a civic sermon and that it is the twentieth century's Sermon on the Mount. In this instance, King chooses to make our entire nation and the world accountable to bring their offering to the altar and make brotherly and sisterly reconciliation. "It is obvious today that America has defaulted on this promissory note in so far as her citizens of color are concerned. Instead of honoring this sacred obligation, America has given the Negro people a bad check; a check which has come back marked 'insufficient funds.'"[10] But this is the twenty-first century, and still, people of African descent wait for fellow members of our human family to hold themselves responsible and accountable; namely, dominating classes' personal and ethical behavior is to reconcile with deserving communities.

In a similar fashion, it appears that Charles P. Henry reinterprets King's "I Have a Dream" as a civic sermon. Accordingly, King's sermon focuses on reconciliation and more narrowly on economic restitution. In addition, Henry, the author of *Long Overdue*, sees King's civic sermon as the catalyst for what has been described earlier as a new consciousness and a cultural paradigm shift, a consciousness and shift that guides all toward understanding that reconciliation is a human justice movement that results in economic restitution or economic reparations.

Henry summarizes King's strategy to infuse a new cultural consciousness and create an economic paradigm shift. King then is intentional in "I Have a Dream." By way of metaphor, King opens our collective consciousness in order to recognize deeper meaning. That is, the call from people of African descent for economic justice has emerged. This is at the heart of Henry's commentary that rightly provides a historical context for the metaphor "I Have a Dream." The following excerpts, by first King (quoted in Henry) and then Henry himself, make this point saliently clear:

> It is a constitutional right for a man to be able to vote but the human right to a decent house is as categorically imperative and morally absolute as was that constitutional right. It is not a constitutional right that men have jobs, but it is a human right.[11]

As early as 1960 King used a version of the "dream" metaphor that included economic rights. The dream encompassed "equality of opportunity, of privilege and prosperity widely distributed; a dream of a land where men will not take necessities from the many to give luxuries to the few." Indeed, the slogan of the 1963 March on Washington was "jobs and freedom." After the Watts riot, King was saying that freedom was not free and was meaningless without the economic means to pursue it. As Ella Baker put it, "The movement was bigger than a hamburger."[12]

The first brief statement was made by King. The purpose of its inclusion is to compare and contrast differences in constitutional and human rights. I characterize these constitutional rights as biased assumptions that reinforce Eurocentric supremacy which insulates hegemonic ideals and rules that protect the ruling classes. These rules hedge our elites from otherness. King prophetically calls these assumptions into question; that is, how do we derive what are our constitutional rights and what is their *raison d'etre*?

In King's view, the nation's constitutional rights do not reinforce universal human rights. If the framers of the Constitution did understand what King concluded, certainly they did not accept his views of constitutional and human rights. I agree with King; people of African descent and color are equal to white men and women. For this reason, the sociopolitical, economic, and psychological contexts that surround the Constitution's fundamental premise suggest that it is not an ethical document. If it is not ethical, it points toward an immoral and inhuman pathology.

King's public addresses and writings made clear what was privately known by some of his closest advisors: a new consciousness and a paradigm shift were required.[13] The civil rights movement then hurried toward including and even highlighting a human rights agenda. What is more, Henry has provided a point of departure in order that we may reconsider reconciliation as a human justice motif. Furthermore, I add that when reconciliation is understood as a justice motif, economic reparations follow. Second, a justice motif reveals that reconciliation is a biblical mandate. In their wholeness, these three—reconciliation, justice, and economic reparations—make a strong case for the word of reconciliation.

Defining the Word of Reconciliation

It is important to define what I mean by the word of reconciliation. Let us begin with the apostle Paul:

> From now on, therefore, we regard no one from a human point of view; even though we once knew Christ from a human point of view, we know him no longer in that way. So if anyone is in Christ, there is a new creation: everything old has passed away; see, everything has become new! All this is from God, who reconciled us to himself through Christ, and has given us the ministry of reconciliation; that is, in Christ God was reconciling the world to himself, not counting their trespasses against them, and entrusting the message [literally, "word"] of reconciliation to us. So we are ambassadors for Christ, since God is making his appeal through us; we entreat you on behalf of Christ, be reconciled to God. (2 Corinthians 5:16-20, NRSV)

What does Paul mean by "reconciliation"? In 2 Corinthians 5:18 we read that "God, who reconciled (καταλλάξαντος; *katallasso*) us to himself through Christ," gave us "the ministry of reconciliation" (διακονίαν τῆς καταλλαγῆς; *diakonian* tēs katallagēs). We read in 2 Corinthians 5:19, "Christ was reconciling (καταλλάσσων; *katallassōn*) the world to himself," and "he has committed to us the word of reconciliation" (λόγον τῆς καταλλαγῆς; *logon tēs katallagēs*). Notice the syntactical pattern: reconciled (v. 18a), reconciliation (v. 18b), reconciling (v. 19a), and reconciliation (v. 19c) in a final form. And in verse 20, Paul writes, "be reconciled to God" (καταλλάγητε; *katallagēte*).[14]

In 2 Corinthians 5:16-20, the apostle Paul intentionally employs the word *reconciliation* in different verb tenses, syntax, and strategy. With different verb tenses, Paul recreates the human journey that includes implicitly the humanly depraved fall from God's grace. Paul is brilliant in his storyline development of human failure and our human need to repent and doggedly pursue the justice motif that is inherent in word of reconciliation. In verse 18, Paul writes that it is "God who reconciled us," the verb tense indicating an action that has occurred, is occurring, and will still occur in the future.[15] The verb may be translated as "having reconciled."

In verse 18b, Paul uses the word *reconciliation* as a gentle possessive noun.[16] In short, reconciliation is something that is to be claimed. In verse

19a, Paul writes that "God was in Christ reconciling the world to himself."[17] Reconciliation may be interpreted as a manifestation or an incarnation into the world through Christ. Reconciliation here points toward the subject, which is Christ. In verse 19c, "reconciliation" is expressed as the "word of reconciliation." This too may be interpreted as something possessed or something to be held in stewardship. This may mean that persons or a person may need to make a judgment or judgments.[18]

In verse 20c, Paul makes what appears to be a final appeal, "be reconciled." Paul and others ("we") believe that it is an imperative that the nature of Christ takes hold on us. It is then an ethical imperative that we are gripped by a new consciousness and a paradigm shift, and we become members of his new community. In short, we are God's redeemed people, who find ways to reconcile with brothers and sisters in community.[19]

What have we discovered by this brief syntactical word study? Paul expresses *reconciliation* in five moves. We can narrow our findings to the following words. First, reconciliation is ongoing (v. 18b). Second, reconciliation (v. 18c) is possessive and a claim. Third, reconciliation (v. 19a) is a manifestation of God's presence, an incarnation of Christ. Fourth, reconciliation (v. 19c) is responsible, and an accountable stewardship of ministry. Fifth, reconciliation (v. 20c) is not an alternative. Instead, it is a command from the Lord.[20]

Therefore, I conclude that in our study of 2 Corinthians 5:16-20, Paul's verb tenses, syntax, and strategy provide an accurate interpretation. Reconciliation is meant to be understood as transactional. It is "change or exchange" (*allaso*; *allasso*). We can create word pictures to illustrate. First, we notice two or more parties in a marketplace. They engage in price negations over goods or services. The equal parties understand communal polity. (I say equal because both are influenced by God's kingdom principles.) These women negotiate a price for "change and exchange" of their goods or services. Once the price is settled, it is binding, and therefore the women are reconciled.

A second word picture is a courtroom setting with a jury (an ecclesial courtroom and jury because these parties are influenced by God's kingdom principles). A party or parties, the plaintiff, alleges injurious behavior against the defendant. The ruling is that the defendant is found guilty and therefore must "change or exchange" to reconcile. The plaintiff may believe his or her award is not large enough, but it is decided that the assigned amount is reasonable in light of the determined damage which has caused the injury or injuries.

The defendant might believe that the awarded amount is too large, but it is settled by the assigned stewards over this ministry to judge, rule, and impose these ramifications to satisfy, support, and reinforce that human justice is a central part of the word of reconciliation. Once the parties leave the courtroom, they might not agree with the justice motif, but it is binding. This is our understanding of reconciliation. Furthermore, it is important to remind readers that my application is plausible if the parties involved are considered equally human and that no other political, socioeconomic, or psychological biases are taken into consideration. But does this formulation hold its own water with Eurocentric assumptions?

Salvific Implications of Reconciliation

I turn to Alexander Maclaren, considered one of the darlings of the Victorian British pulpit, whose exposition of Scripture appears in a seventeen-volume set.[21] When Maclaren expounded upon 2 Corinthians 5:17, he employed Jeremiah 13:23 and Revelation 21:5 to buttress his explanation for what he believed reconciliation means. The former reads, "Can the Ethiopian change his skin or the leopard his spots? Then you also can do good who are accustomed to doing evil" (Jeremiah 13:23, NASB). The latter reads, "And He who sits on the throne said, 'Behold, I am making all things new.' And He said, 'Write, for these words are faithful and true'" (Revelation 21:5, NASB). Maclaren then writes,

> We note the picturesque rhetorical question here. They were occasionally accustomed to see the dark-skinned, Ethiopian, whether we suppose that these were true negroes from Southern Egypt or dark Arabs, and now and then leopards came up from the thickets on the Jordan, or from the hills of the southern wilderness about the Dead Sea. The black hue of the man, the dark spots that starred the skin of the fierce beast, are fitting emblems of the evil that dyes and speckles the soul. Whether it wraps the whole character in black, or whether it only spots it here and there with tawny yellow, it is ineradicable; and a man can no more change his character once formed than a negro can cast his skin, or a leopard whiten out the spots on his hide.

Now we do not need to assert that a man has no power of self-improvement or reformation. The exhortations of the prophet to repentance and to cleansing imply that he has. If he has not, then it is no blame to him that he does not mend. Experience shows that we have a very considerable power of such a kind. It is a pity that some Christian teachers speak in exaggerated terms about the impossibility of such self-improvement.

But it is very difficult.[22]

Maclaren's comments are ghostly white and uncomely. His commentary does not leave much to the imagination about his Eurocentric worldview, his cultural biases, and his racism against people of African descent. If Maclaren's commentary is to be considered seriously in the twenty-first century, it is very difficult. This is an example of how a respected and sometimes revered academic preacher was influenced by his cultural worldview that hindered his exposition and, in this instance, quite possibly his understanding of reconciliation.

Perhaps Maclaren's perspective of reconciliation was conditioned by European colonialism, which is empire. Philosophically, empire functions through class distinctions (politics, economics) and race manipulations. "Empires [Egypt, Assyria, Babylon, Persia, Greece, and Rome] enforce and maintain domination over oppressed peoples through military might, economic oppression, and ideological belief systems, no matter what era of history they may emerge."[23]

Moreover, in Maclaren's world, people of African descent were not considered to be equally human, and therefore I find it difficult to believe that Maclaren would have thought it important to avoid empire's hegemonic colonial influences over his exposition or theology. We know that empire blurs cultural lines between dominating cultural spheres such as religion, politics, and economics, similar to W. E. B. Du Bois's construct of race, economics, and politics.[24]

Instead, empire is used to cloak and hide demonic powers of empire that are beneath the veil. Unware people are manipulated to support and slavishly serve these very systems that are not in their best interest. Maclaren cannot be considered as a proponent of a radicalized and revolutionary gospel and the word of reconciliation. Twenty-first-century Du Bosian preachers, however, must; these preachers doggedly pursue the ethical imperative of the twenty-first century, which is closing the income and wealth inequality gaps.[25]

Therefore reconciliation must be defined as our radical pursuit of human justice. For our example, we look no further than to Jesus. Jesus of Nazareth was radicalized by the Holy Spirit, and those who follow him share his radicalized nature. Those radicalized by the gospel and the Holy Spirit are co-agents and co-agitators who understand and accept and make efforts to eradicate human inequalities. We see income and wealth inequalities as a demonic stronghold of empire. Twenty-first-century reconciliation is radical, because it calls those radicalized by Jesus to seek ways to abolish human disenfranchisement. Did the apostle Paul share this radicalized understanding of reconciliation?

I believe that he did. I also believe that Eurocentric theologians, pastors, and others have not fully considered the apostle Paul and his full expression of the word of reconciliation. To do so, we must recognize that Paul was radicalized by his encounter with the risen Jesus (Acts 9:1-9; 26:12-23). Paul was assigned to marshal both reconciliation between God and humanity and humanity with humanity. It is in the latter that Eurocentric theology and ideology languishes. To fully commit to reconciling humanity with humanity requires a sense that all humanity is equally human.

What is necessary then is a definition that explains reconciliation is radical and doggedly pursued by those who have been radicalized by Jesus' ethic. Allan Boesak and Curtiss Paul DeYoung provide this kind of perspective in *Radical Reconciliation*. In this instance, DeYoung writes in the chapter "Reconciliation in the Empire" a radicalized definition for reconciliation:

> The word *reconciliation* appears occasionally in the New Testament and, with a few exceptions, always in the Pauline literature. The word translates several related Greek words: the verbs *katallassō* and *apokatallassō* and the noun *katallagē*. These words were utilized by Greek writers to discuss interpersonal relationships. In particular, they were used in peace treaties between nations and groups. So, in common Greek usage, there were very often political dimensions to the meaning of reconciliation. When Jewish scholars translated the Hebrew scriptures into Greek, they used these words to translate the Hebrew words

related to atonement—that is, to God being reconciled with humanity. In this usage of *katallassō,* they did not retain the political dimension found in the Greek understanding of reconciliation. On the other hand, when Greek writers used the words, they never implied a spiritual connotation to reconciliation. In Paul's use of *katallassō* and related terms, we find both the spiritual and political meanings. His readership, both Greeks and Jews, would have understood reconciliation in this way as they discussed his letters in their gatherings.[26]

De Young goes further:

> *Katallassō* means literally, "to change or exchange; to effect a change." . . . Reconciliation is a process that causes us to overcome "alienation through identification and in solidarity with 'the other,' thus making peace and restoring relationships." . . . Reconciliation can be understood as exchanging places with 'the other,' overcoming alienation through identification, solidarity, restoring relationships, positive change, new frameworks, and a rich togetherness that is both spiritual and political."[27]

And I add that radical reconciliation is to "change or exchange" social location to fight for what is to be morally and humanly ethical and legal.

Whether it is the apostle Paul, or how Dr. King understands Jesus' ethic, or De Young, all see reconciliation as a radicalized idea that shapes our human consciousness. "Reconciliation is radical in that it reaches to the very roots of injustice. Paul understood that injustice creates the need for reconciliation. Therefore reconciliation is about [human] social justice."[28] De Young provides depth to our understanding and grasp of Paul's original vision for the word of reconciliation. The following excerpt further adds to our understanding that reconciliation is salvific but includes a human justice motif:

> Reconciliation is a real experience that is radical, going to the roots of injustice. Reconciliation is also revolutionary. Theologian Gustavo Gutiérrez writes that revolution means "abolish the present status quo and attempt to replace it with a qualitatively different one." Ephesians 2 says that Jesus created "in himself one new humanity in place of the two, thus making peace, and might reconcile both groups to God in one

body through the cross" (2:15b-16a). The passage seems to be saying that in place of two categories of humanity—powerful Romans and oppressed Jews (along with other colonized people)—a qualitatively different understanding of humanity was implemented. Ephesians 2 calls for a revolution of human identity. It signals to us that apartheid, Jim Crow, patriarchy, class status, and other systemic forms of classifying humanity for domination are being replaced by a new structure of "one new humanity" through Jesus' death on a cross and resurrection.[29]

Reconciliation then is a lived experience: "having reconciled" or "be reconciled" (2 Corinthians 5:18-19). As human inequality increases, the illuminating light of the Holy Spirit shines and causes we who follow Jesus to lament, critique, and protest the inequalities which are inconsistent with Jesus' ethic (Matthew 5–7). Thus Jesus' followers are compelled to find more radical solutions to increasingly hostile conflicts among the world's populations; we seek peace among God and humanity and humanity with humanity. I agree with DeYoung; reconciliation is revolutionary at its taproot. What is more, reconciliation usurps the demonic power of hegemony—the source of empire's power.

Conclusion

Dr. King's "I Have a Dream" points us toward moral, ethical, and legal human failures. This civic sermon also makes us aware that dangers are inherent in our blind trust in Eurocentrism and its cultural beliefs, values, and mythologies that include white privilege. For centuries white privilege has reinforced and provided undue advantages. To remedy this sin, it will take enormous courage to acknowledge and accept that this is human failure. It will take enormous courage to accept that white privilege has caused ghastly damage to our collective human psyche. It begins with the apostle Paul's declaration that we "be reconciled" (2 Corinthians 5:20), which is an admission of corporate and collective guilt and culpability.

At the same time, King's civic sermon demands that the oppressor make economic restitution to the oppressed. King, indeed, grounds his demand in an informed understanding of Pauline theology and Paul's explanation of the word of reconciliation and Jesus' ethic. It is clear, furthermore, that Jesus' ethic is the seedbed for King's "beloved community," which is a euphemism for the principles of the kingdom of God that are presented in the Sermon on the Mount (Matthew 5–7).[30] As earlier mentioned, I consider "I Have a Dream" to be the twentieth century's Sermon on the Mount. King adroitly appropriates that sermon and makes it his own. He employs the setting of that historical event and occasion and then applies it to his contemporary rhetorical situation in order to shape and craft his civic sermon.

What is more, King's "I Have a Dream" civic sermon is a re-presentation of the word of reconciliation. King's rhetorical goal is to make clear that the word of reconciliation is broad and complex. It is more than God reconciling to humanity through the ignominious death of Jesus on a cross. Jesus' death includes humanity reconciling with humanity. It is my view that we cannot have one without the other. For this to be realized, those who enjoy economic and racial privilege must truly love Jesus' ethic and comply with the apostle Paul's demand in 2 Corinthians 5:16-20. It is imperative that the privileged seek exorcism from the demonic strongholds and the suffocating power of empire. The word of reconciliation requires that the powerful let go of the grip of materialism. This can happen only when the powerful embrace God's kingdom principles that also inform the apostle Paul's charge.

Jesus' ethic and a Pauline theological explanation of the original intent of the word of reconciliation are counterintuitive to the ideological entrapments that inform Eurocentrism. This ideology lies at the taproot of Western culture and civilization and supports Eurocentric thought that evolves into this demonic ideology. Among other things, Eurocentric–demonic ideology then has a grip over theology and exposition. Earlier in this chapter, there is a brief but gravely disappointing example of this demonic theology and exposition located in Alexander Maclaren's unimpressive explanation of the word of reconciliation in 2 Corinthians 5:16-20.

Theology and exposition matter intensely because each has unlimited influence over what Eurocentric societies hold to be true; therefore, it shapes our socioeconomic, sociopolitical, and psychospiritual pathologies. Whether it is an appreciation of Pauline theology or Jesus' ethic, it is demanded from all to reconsider what the word of reconciliation means.

Throughout this chapter, I have made a concerted effort to do just that. What follows in chapter 5 is an attempt to reframe our argument for reparations by analyzing the Jewish model, which has three major parts, namely, a collective liberation narrative and a simultaneous human justice movement that results in economic reparations.

NOTES

1. Martin Luther King, Jr., "I Have a Dream," *A Testament of Hope: The Essential of Martin Luther King, Jr.,* ed. James M. Washington (New York: HarperCollin, 1991), 217.

2. Don Lipman, "A Day to Remember: August 28, 1963—What Was Weather Like for MLK Dream Speech?", *Washington Post* (August 24, 2011). See https://www.washingtonpost.com/blogs/capital-weather-gang/post/a-day-to-remember-august-28-1963/2011/08/24/gIQADeZZbJ_blog.html?utm_term=.16c3284cdefc, accessed June 6, 2017.

3. King, "I Have a Dream," *A Testament of Hope,* 217.

4. Cornel West, *Democracy Matters: Winning the Fight Against Imperialism* (New York: Penguin, 2004), 22.

5. Ibid.

6. Wyatt Tee Walker in "Our Poor People's Campaign," which is the second chapter of this book (35–39).

7. See Howard Schultz, *Onward: How Starbucks Fought for Its Life Without Losing Its Soul* (New York: Rodale Books, 2011). Starbucks claims that "99% of our coffee is ethically sourced." See "Ethical Sourcing: Coffee," https://www.starbucks.com/responsibility/sourcing/coffee, accessed June 6, 2017.

8. Lewis Baldwin, *To Make the Wounded Whole: A Cultural Legacy of Martin Luther King Jr.* (Minneapolis: Augsburg Fortress, 1992), 1.

9. This brief summary of the Sermon on the Mount and the headings are my own.

10. King, "I Have a Dream," 217.

11. King, quoted in Charles P. Henry, *Long Overdue: The Politics of Racial Reparations* (New York: New York University Press, 2007), 58.

12. Henry, 58.

13. See Walker, "Our Poor People's Campaign," 35–39.

14. I have used Richard J. Goodrich and Albert L. Lukaszewski, eds., *A Reader's Greek New Testament,* 2nd ed. (Grand Rapids: Zondervan, 2007), 387–88.

15. *A Reader's Greek New Testament* has copious exegetical notes and commentary on each chapter included on each page just beneath the original

Koine Greek text. The verb used in 2 Corinthians 5:18 is an aorist participle, active genitive, and masculine singular.

16. In 2 Corinthians 5:18b, the word *reconciliation* is genitive and feminine singular in form. See *A Reader's Greek New Testament.*

17. In 2 Corinthians 19a, "reconciliation" is rendered as "reconciling." It is a present participle, active nominative, and masculine singular in form. See ibid.

18. In 2 Corinthians 5:19c, "reconciliation" is translated as a noun, genitive feminine singular. See ibid.

19. In verse 20c, Paul makes what appears to be a final appeal, "be reconciled." It is translated as an aorist imperative, and a passive second person plural. See ibid.

20. Ibid.

21. William H. Willimon and Richard Lischer, eds., *Concise Encyclopedia of Preaching* (Louisville: Westminster John Knox, 1995). Maclaren was born in Glasgow, Scotland, in 1836, and educated at Glasgow University and Stepney College, which today is the University of London (316).

22. Alexander Maclaren, "An Impossibility Made Possible," in *Expositions of Holy Scripture: Isaiah and Jeremiah* (Grand Rapids: Baker Books, 1984), 275.

23. Allan Aubrey Boesak and Curtiss Paul DeYoung, *Radical Reconciliation: Beyond Political Pietism and Christian Quietism* (Maryknoll, NY: Orbis Books, 2016), 12–13. To Boesak and DeYoung's list of empires, I would add Great Britain and the United States.

24. See W. E. B. Du Bois, *Dusk of Dawn: An Essay Toward an Autobiography of a Race Concept* (Piscataway, NJ: Transaction Publishers, 2011), 129.

25. Thomas Piketty, *Capital in the Twenty-First Century* (Cambridge, MA: The Belknap Press of Harvard University Press, 2014), 1.

26. Boesak and DeYoung, *Radical Reconciliation*, 11–12.

27. Ibid., 12.

28. Ibid., 18.

29. Ibid., 19.

30. Martin Luther King Jr., *Where Do We Go from Here: Chaos or Community?* (Boston: Beacon Press, 1968), xi.

Excursus
Apology and Reconciliation

Recently, Georgetown University, a leading American Eurocentric institution of higher education, made a startling admission. The university admitted that it had benefitted economically through selling some of the university's slaves to save the school. This may mean that the injured descendants of the enslaved men and women will be awarded large sums of restitution and reparations:

> One hundred and seventy-nine years ago, two Jesuit priests sold 272 persons at a slave auction. Their families were torn apart: Many of them were shipped more than 1,000 miles to Louisiana, and many more were barred from practicing their Catholic faith by new slave masters. Meanwhile, the Jesuit priests used the money they received from the sale to pay off debts for Georgetown University, the oldest Catholic university in the United States. On April 18 [2017], Georgetown University and the Maryland Jesuits apologized for their roles in the slave sale and started their ongoing efforts to make amends for their actions. On Thursday [April 17, 2017], the university's president, John DeGioia, apologized for the school's historical involvement in the slave trade. Father Timothy Kesicki, president of the Jesuit Conference of Canada and the United States, made an . . . apology to God and the descendants of the 272 slaves sold by the Maryland Jesuits.[1]

It is important to grasp what is meant by an apology. A Eurocentric apology in a public sphere may mean something different than it seems on the surface. Deeper observation and study may disclose that an apology is a defense of one's actions and not an admission of one's guilt.

The Example of Socrates

A Eurocentric example is that of Plato, who wrote *Socrates' Defense (Apology)*. We will do well to remember that Plato's Socrates did not admit his personal guilt. This Greek text is an influential literary contribution to the so-called Western canon. Among other things, this literary piece serves as a philosophical form for how to execute a successful legal defense in Western culture. However, *Socrates' Defense (Apology)* is not a philosophical example of spiritual contrition.[2] To understand a traditional view of the *Apology*, I have appropriated the outline of scholars Edward P. J. Corbett and Robert J. Connors:

1. Socrates' introductionary remarks to the assembly (paragraph 1).

2. Narratio—the statement of the charges (paragraph 2).

3. Refutation of the old charges (paragraphs 3–12).

4. Refutation of the recent charges—Socrates' cross-examination of Meletus (paragraphs 13–53).

5. Concluding remarks (paragraph 54).[3]

In addition, Corbett and Connors explain that Socrates' *Apology* is a species of judicial rhetoric which is frequently exercised in a courtroom. It can be employed, however, in an "extra-courtroom" defense or context. "If we understand the term *apologize* in its Greek sense 'to defend' and the term *categorize* in its Greek sense of 'accuse,' we have two terms that most aptly describe the basic functions of judicial discourse."[4] Corbett and Connors help to shape our modern understanding of an ancient rhetorical tool, commonly used as a defense against legal and moral charges.

Readers remember that Socrates was accused of corrupting the minds of the youth of Athens. He was accused by the Athenian elites. Socrates, in his defense, did not say that he was sorry; he did not ask for forgiveness; he did not admit that he was wrong:

No doubt you think, gentlemen, that I have been condemned for lack of the arguments which I could have used if I had thought it right to leave nothing unsaid or undone to secure my acquittal. But that is very far from the truth. It is not a lack of arguments that caused me condemnation, but a lack of effrontery and impudence, and the fact I have refused to address you in the way which would give you most pleasure. You would have liked to hear me weep and wail, doing and saying all sorts of things which I regard as unworthy of myself, but which you are used to hearing from other people. But I did not think then that I ought to stoop to servility because I was in danger, and I do not regret now the way in which I pleaded my case. I would much rather die as the result of this defense than live as the result of the other sort. In a court of law, just as in warfare, neither I nor any other ought to use his wits to escape death by any means. In battle it is often obvious that you could escape being killed by giving up your arms and throwing yourself upon the mercy of your pursuers, and in every kind of danger there are plenty of devices for avoiding death if you are un-scrupulous enough to stick at nothing. But I suggest, gentlemen, that the difficulty is to escape from doing wrong; which is far more fleet of foot. In this present instance I, the slow old man, have been overtaken by the slower of the two, but my accusers, who are clever and quick, have been overtaken by the faster—by iniquity. When I leave this court I shall go condemned by you to death, but they will go away convicted by truth herself of depravity and wickedness. And they accept their sentence even as I accept mine. No doubt it was bound to be so, and I think that the result is fair enough.[5]

This passage from *Socrates' Defense (Apology)* is an example of what can be gained by unfamiliar and uninformed listeners when we gather to listen to a Georgetown University–like public apology. An oppressor may ask for forgiveness from the oppressed but never admit that she or he is wrong. Oppressors may admit that they were morally reprehensi-ble, but many never admit they are legally liable to reward damages. In their defense, their actions were quite immoral and unethical at the time of their offense against you; but unfortunately, their actions were quite legal at the time that it occurred.

The Example of William Clinton Regarding
the Tuskegee Experiment

William Jefferson Clinton, then president of the United States, made an apology to family members of the men of the Tuskegee experiment. The experiment was an immoral and inhumane egregious act. "Clinton's apology was made to those survivors of the government-sponsored Tuskegee experiment, in which scientists with the U.S. Public Health Service used 399 poor black men with syphilis as guinea pigs."[6] Scientists from the United States government blatantly lied to these men and their families about their prognosis and diagnostic treatment. In fact, for the experiment to be effectively measurable, these men of African descent were left to die so that these immoral and unethical scientists would be able to prove their hypothesis. Of Clinton's apology, the following excerpt is a part of an editorial written in the Orlando *Sun Sentinel*:

> Saying "I am sorry" is the least President Clinton can do for victims of an evil, horrifying and morally reprehensible government plot. He bears no personal responsibility for shocking decades-old deeds. But he is rightly assuming a moral obligation to express official regret and trying to bring closure to this open wound in American history. His apology will have great symbolic meaning for black people, some who are not entirely convinced that institutional government racism is a thing of the past.[7]

If we apply our Socratic definition of an apology alongside the editorial writer's opinion, we are able to understand that Clinton's apology is not a legally binding admission of culpability on the part of the United States government. Instead, it is part memorial (in memoriam) and part restorative justice.

For now, it is important to outline Clinton's apology. Like Corbett's and Connors's outline for Socrates's *Apology*, Clinton's apology is divided under their five major headings. I have determined, however, that Clinton's apology has approximately twenty paragraphs.[8] As mentioned, the divisions in Clinton's apology are similar to those of Corbett and Connors. First, Clinton's Socratic introduction is paragraphs 1–3. Second, Clinton's Socratic narratio (narrative in brief)—the statement of the charges—is paragraphs 4–7. Third, Clinton's Socratic refutation of old charges is paragraph 8. Fourth, Clinton's Socratic refutation of recent charges—Socrates's [and Clinton's self-] cross examination—is paragraphs 9–17. Fifth, Clinton's Socratic concluding remarks are paragraphs 18–20).

In paragraph 9, it is clear that Clinton expresses his sense of personal moral guilt; it is not, however, a clear admission that the United States government is legally responsible. In short, there was no reward of individual economic restitution to any of the men abused—that is, the injured parties. Note that in paragraph 11, Clinton issues a vague apology. In paragraphs 11–17, I suggest the actions taken by the United States government may be interpreted as "restorative justice."[9]

Clinton's Socratic Introduction (paragraphs 1–3)

[1] THE PRESIDENT: Ladies and gentlemen, on Sunday, Mr. Shaw will celebrate his 95th birthday. I would like to recognize the other survivors who are here today and their families: Mr. Charlie Pollard is here. Mr. Carter Howard. Mr. Fred Simmons. Mr. Simmons just took his first airplane ride, and he reckons he's about 110 years old, so I think it's time for him to take a chance or two. I'm glad he did. And Mr. Frederick Moss, thank you, sir.

[2] I would also like to ask three family representatives who are here— Sam Doner is represented by his daughter, Gwendolyn Cox. Thank you, Gwendolyn. Ernest Hendon, who is watching in Tuskegee, is represented by his brother, North Hendon. Thank you, sir, for being here. And George Key is represented by his grandson, Christopher Monroe. Thank you, Chris.

[3] I also acknowledge the families, community leaders, teachers and students watching today by satellite from Tuskegee. The White House is the people's house; we are glad to have all of you here today. I thank Dr. David Satcher for his role in this. I thank Congresswoman Waters and Congressman Hilliard, Congressman Stokes, the entire Congressional Black Caucus. Dr. Satcher, members of the Cabinet who are here, Secretary Herman, Secretary Slater. A great friend of freedom, Fred Gray, [I] thank you for fighting this long battle all these long years.

Clinton's Socratic Narratio: Statement of the Charges (paragraphs 4–7)

[4] The eight men who are survivors of the syphilis study at Tuskegee are a living link to a time not so very long ago that many Americans would prefer not to remember, but we dare not forget. It was a time when our nation failed to live up to its ideals, when our nation broke the trust with our people that is the very foundation of our democracy. It is not only in remembering that shameful past that we can make amends and repair our nation, but it is in remembering that past that we can build a better present and a better future. And without remembering it, we cannot make amends and we cannot go forward.

[5] So today America does remember the hundreds of men used in research without their knowledge and consent. We remember them and their family members. Men who were poor and African American, without resources and with few alternatives, they believed they had found hope when they were offered free medical care by the United States Public Health Service. They were betrayed.

[6] Medical people are supposed to help when we need care, but even once a cure was discovered, they were denied help, and they were lied to by their government. Our government is supposed to protect the rights of its citizens; their rights were trampled upon. Forty years, hundreds of men betrayed, along with their wives and children, along with the community in Macon County, Alabama, the City of Tuskegee, the fine university there, and the larger African American community.

[7] The United States government did something that was wrong— deeply, profoundly, [and] morally wrong. It was an outrage to our commitment to integrity and equality for all our citizens.

Clinton's Socratic Refutation of Old Charges (paragraph 8)

[8] To the survivors, to the wives and family members, the children and the grandchildren, I say what you know: No power on Earth can give you back the lives lost, the pain suffered, the years of internal torment and anguish. What was done cannot be undone. But we can end the

silence. We can stop turning our heads away. We can look at you in the eye and finally say on behalf of the American people, what the United States government did was shameful, and I am sorry. The American people are sorry—for the loss, for the years of hurt. You did nothing wrong, but you were grievously wronged. I apologize and I am sorry that this apology has been so long in coming.

Clinton's Socratic Refutation of Recent Charges: Clinton's Remedies under Self-cross examination and Public Examination (paragraphs 9–17)

[9] To Macon County, to Tuskegee, to the doctors who have been wrongly associated with the events there, you have our apology, as well. To our African American citizens, I am sorry that your federal government orchestrated a study so clearly racist. That can never be allowed to happen again. It is against everything our country stands for and what we must stand against is what it was.

[10] So let us resolve to hold forever in our hearts and minds the memory of a time not long ago in Macon County, Alabama, so that we can always see how adrift we can become when the rights of any citizens are neglected, ignored and betrayed. And let us resolve here and now to move forward together.

[11] The legacy of the study at Tuskegee has reached far and deep, in ways that hurt our progress and divide our nation. We cannot be one America when a whole segment of our nation has no trust in America. An apology is the first step, and we take it with a commitment to rebuild that broken trust. We can begin by making sure there is never again another episode like this one.

[12] We need to do more to ensure that medical research practices are sound and ethical, and that researchers work more closely with communities.

[13] Today I would like to announce several steps to help us achieve these goals. First, we will help to build that lasting memorial at Tuskegee. The school founded by Booker T. Washington, distinguished by the renowned scientist George Washington Carver and so many others

who advanced the health and well-being of African Americans and all Americans, is a fitting site. The Department of Health and Human Services will award a planning grant so the school can pursue establishing a center for bioethics in research and health care. The center will serve as a museum of the study and support efforts to address its legacy and strengthen bioethics training.

[14] Second, we commit to increase our community involvement so that we may begin restoring lost trust. The study at Tuskegee served to sow distrust of our medical institutions, especially where research is involved. Since the study was halted, abuses have been checked by making informed consent and local review mandatory in federally-funded and mandated research.

[15] Still, 25 years later, many medical studies have little African American participation and African American organ donors are few. This impedes efforts to conduct promising research and to provide the best health care to all our people, including African Americans. So today, I'm directing the Secretary of Health and Human Services, Donna Shalala, to issue a report in 180 days about how we can best involve communities, especially minority communities, in research and health care. You must—every American group must be involved in medical research in ways that are positive. We have put the curse behind us; now we must bring the benefits to all Americans.

[16] Third, we commit to strengthen researchers' training in bioethics. We are constantly working on making breakthroughs in protecting the health of our people and in vanquishing diseases. But all our people must be assured that their rights and dignity will be respected as new drugs, treatments and therapies are tested and used. So I am directing Secretary Shalala to work in partnership with higher education to prepare training materials for medical researchers. They will be available in a year. They will help researchers build on core ethical principles of respect for individuals, justice and informed consent, and advise them on how to use these principles effectively in diverse populations.

[17] Fourth, to increase and broaden our understanding of ethical issues and clinical research, we commit to providing postgraduate fellowships

to train bioethicists especially among African Americans and other minority groups. HHS will offer these fellowships beginning in September of 1998 to promising students enrolled in bioethics graduate programs.

Clinton's Socratic Concluding Remarks (paragraphs 18–20)

[18] And, finally, by executive order I am also today extending the charter of the National Bioethics Advisory Commission to October of 1999. The need for this commission is clear. We must be able to call on the thoughtful, collective wisdom of experts and community representatives to find ways to further strengthen our protections for subjects in human research.

[19] We face a challenge in our time. Science and technology are rapidly changing our lives with the promise of making us much healthier, much more productive and more prosperous. But with these changes we must work harder to see that as we advance we don't leave behind our conscience. No ground is gained and, indeed, much is lost if we lose our moral bearings in the name of progress.

[20] The people who ran the study at Tuskegee diminished the stature of man by abandoning the most basic ethical precepts. They forgot their pledge to heal and repair. They had the power to heal the survivors and all the others and they did not. Today, all we can do is apologize. But you have the power, for only you—Mr. Shaw, the others who are here, the family members who are with us in Tuskegee—only you have the power to forgive. Your presence here shows us that you have chosen a better path than your government did so long ago. You have not withheld the power to forgive. I hope today and tomorrow every American will remember your lesson and live by it. Thank you and God bless you.[10]

In summary, Clinton's apology concedes that these people of African descent were abused and mistreated. He concedes that the abuses and mistreatments were immoral and unethical actions sanctioned by the United States government. Clinton does not concede that these infected and affected people of African descent should receive economic reparations individually.

How then were their families compensated? How were the families restored? Was restorative justice appropriate without retribution—economic justice? Does Clinton willingly ignore the essence of King's "I Have a Dream" civic sermon in which King declared that "America has given the Negro people a bad check, a check which has come back marked 'insufficient funds'"?[11]

Indeed, Clinton did offer a personal apology (paragraph 9), but was and is that enough? The apology was his alone. Although Clinton was head of state, his apology did not clearly point solely to the guilt and responsibility of the United States government. In paragraph 6, Clinton's remarks become vague and open to legal interpretation, pointing toward the medical officers and their breach of ethics. In short, a financial remuneration may be against the physicians and their healthcare teams: "Medical people are supposed to help when we need care, but even once a cure was discovered, they were denied help, and they were lied to by their government." Reading Clinton's apology in this way, all recognized that Clinton leaves rhetorical space to recuse the United States government from punitive damages.

Clinton did provide a corrective to our collective public memory (paragraph 9), but a memorial is only a necessary ceremonial step. Without economic reparations, this does not ensure that such atrocities will not occur again. Clinton's apology then is similar to the recent public apology issued by the officials of Georgetown University. In that case, admitting their moral guilt to God and to the families of the injured plainly is a moral plea, but that admission of guilt to God is not necessarily binding. According to the United States Constitution and state and territorial laws, slavery was not illegal at the time of the offense. What is more, God is not on trial and cannot be in a United States trial. At the time of this writing, we wait for remedies that will result in economic restitution for those injured families.

Charles P. Henry reinforces that we must understand the difference between an apology and a defense. An apology is not necessarily an admission of legal guilt. "An apology does not mean, however, that the dispute is resolved. In most cases, it is only the first step in a reparation process that may involve restitution, compensation, rehabilitation, satisfaction, and guarantees that the action not be repeated."[12] Nor should it be. As mentioned, the presidential apologies of Georgetown University and the United States must end in forms of restitution such as economic reparation.

NOTES

1. Adelaide Mena and Matt Hadro, "Georgetown University Begins to Make Amends for 1838 Sale of 272 Persons," *National Catholic Register*, http://www.ncregister.com/daily-news/georgetown-university-begins-to-make-amends-for-1838-sale-of-272-persons, accessed April 22, 2017.

2. Plato, *The Collected Dialogues of Plato*, ed. Edith Hamilton and Huntington Cairns (Princeton, NJ: Princeton University Press, 1989).

3. Edward P. J. Corbett and Robert J. Connors, *Classical Rhetoric for the Modern Student* (Oxford: Oxford University Press, 1998), 205.

4. Ibid., 204.

5. Ibid., 23.

6. Charles P. Henry, *Long Overdue: The Politics of Racial Reparations* (New York: New York University Press, 2007), 1.

7. *The Sun Sentinel* (Orlando, FL), "Clinton Apology Symbolic, Welcome for Tuskegee Experiment Horrors" (August 14, 1997).

8. William Jefferson Clinton, "Remarks by the President in Apology for [the] Study Done in Tuskegee," delivered from the East Room of the White House, May 16, 1997, 2:26 p.m. EDT; transcript released by the White House, Office of the Press Secretary. The transcript can be found at Centers for Disease Control and Prevention, https://www.cdc.gov/tuskegee/clintonp.htm, accessed May 5, 2017.

9. Clarence J. Munford, *Race and Reparations: A Black Perspective for the 21st Century* (Trenton, NJ: Africa World Press, 1996), 415–39.

10. Clinton, "Remarks by the President."

11. Martin Luther King Jr., "I Have a Dream," *A Testament of Hope: The Essential Writings and Speeches of Martin Luther King, Jr.*, ed. James M. Washington (New York: HarperCollins, 1991), 217–20.

12. Henry, *Long Overdue*, 2.

Passover, Our Collective Liberation Narrative

Exodus 12, Luke 19:1-10, and Shaping a Claim for Justice

The Egyptians urged the people to hasten their departure from the land, for they said, "We shall all be dead." So the people took their dough before it was leavened, with their kneading bowls wrapped up in their cloaks on their shoulders. The Israelites had done as Moses told them; they had asked the Egyptians for jewelry of silver and gold, and for clothing, and the LORD had given the people favor in the sight of the Egyptians, so that they let them have what they asked. So they plundered the Egyptians. (Exodus 12:33-36, NRSV)

This passage from Exodus introduces an emerging collective liberation narrative, a human justice movement that includes economic reparations, and accordingly this broadens our perspective and understanding of the inaugural Passover. In the Passover, we see that justice is urgent; we sense this by the immediate compliance of the dominating Egyptians who resided quite possibly in the vicinity and in intimacy with the Hebrew people when they told the Hebrews to leave or "we shall all be dead" (Exodus 12:33). Also, the Hebrew people immediately complied with Yahweh's demand for justice; they left with their "dough before it was leavened" (Exodus 12:34). For many readers, this is the extent of Passover.

At a closer reading, however, we notice that Yahweh's justice requires more than what we have made into a Christian euphemism. Many contemporary Christians have characterized Passover as personal atonement alone, but it is more: Passover is a justice motif. In short, Yahweh requires human justice. Thus a broader view of Passover discloses the organized presence of a human justice movement that enfleshes specific demands, which is economic reparations. In short, Yahweh's presence manifests into economic restitution.

Later in the emerging Hebrew collective liberation narrative, Yahweh's justice results in the death of Pharaoh and his army at the Sea (Exodus 14:26-28). Historically, Passover is atonement, a covering for sins; in addition, Passover births human resistance to hegemonic empire. Human resistance or a human justice movement then becomes an aegis for what we call a collective liberation narrative. Thereafter, the collective liberation narrative and human justice movement which is Passover remains a recital of how Yahweh agitates his people to advocate for their current and future human rights. We see Passover as an organized movement that demands behavioral or policy changes from empire.

In this way, we read Exodus 12:33-36 as God's justice, made tangible through economic reparations required from and awarded by the dominating Egyptians, the common middle-class Egyptians, and to an extent, the poorest classes of Egyptian people. All Egyptians benefitted from the ruling empire at the expense of the Hebrew slaves. "The Israelites had done as Moses told them; they had asked the Egyptians for jewelry of silver and gold and for clothing, and the Lord had given the people favor in the sight of the Egyptians, so that they let them have what they asked. So they plundered the Egyptians" (Exodus 12:33-35). This justice motif which grounds our collective liberation narrative, human justice movement, and demand for economic reparations continues in the New Testament.

I contend that the writer of Luke's Gospel is aware of and influenced by a similar collective liberation narrative, human justice movement, and claim for economic reparations that I have located previously in Exodus (Exodus 1:8-22; 2:1-10; 6:20; 14:26-28). I further contend that the collective liberation narrative is preunderstood as a part of the Hebrew culture and psyche that is adapted by Hebrew and Jewish characters (Old and New Testaments). Namely, Yahweh is a God of justice who manifests himself as human justice through the human justice movement and thereafter in the awarding of economic reparations. What is more, the collective liberation narrative is a literary invention of an oppressed people. As it is in the Old Testament, so it is in the New Testament: the collective liberation narrative and human justice movement continue to inform and empower the oppressed people to resist empire. One example is located in Luke 19:1-10:

> He entered Jericho and was passing through it. A man was there named Zacchaeus; he was a chief tax collector and was rich. He was trying to see who Jesus was, but on account of the crowd he could not, because he was short in stature. So he ran ahead and climbed a sycamore tree to see him, because he was going to pass that way. When Jesus came to the place, he looked up and said to him, "Zacchaeus, hurry and come down; for I must stay at your house today." So he hurried down and was happy to welcome him. All who saw it began to grumble and said, "He has gone to be the guest of one who is a sinner." Zacchaeus stood there and said to the Lord, "Look, half of my possessions, Lord, I will give to the poor; and if I have defrauded anyone of anything, I will pay back four times as much." Then Jesus said to him, "Today salvation has come to this house, because he too is a son of Abraham. For the Son of Man came [he has come] to seek out and to save the lost." (Luke 19:1-10, NRSV)

At a closer reading, notice this episode's canonical location. Luke 9:27, Luke 15, and Luke 19:45-48 are a canonical thematic pattern. That is, these chapters have a common theme in which Jesus confronts economic inequality while he challenges the Hebrew people to resist empire's luring greed. These chapters foreshadow Jesus' looming and final earthly Passover (Luke 22:1-13). You will see later the significant relationship that Passover has with the shaping of the Hebrew collective liberation narrative, their human justice movement, and its claim for economic reparations.

Luke 15–16 is warning against misguided values; that is, it is sinful to value things more than people. Luke places the Jewish elite into Jesus' audience; they heard clearly his rebuke. The writer places the rich young ruler in Luke 18. The account is significant to all Synoptic writers

(Matthew 19:16-26; Mark 10:17-27; Luke 18:18-23). The episode suggests that Jesus demands that the wealthy young man give (return) to the oppressed his riches, hinting that he extorted the oppressed to become rich. Refusing to do what is moral and ethical, the young man declined to pay reparations. Instead, he chose to side with the rewarding and sanctioning values of greedy empire.

In contrast, we read about Zacchaeus and the parable of money usage in Luke 19:1-27. First we read about Zacchaeus's sinful economic exploitation and his subsequent repentance that requires economic reparations (Luke 19:1-10). Second, we read about an immoral lord who exacted money from the poor (Luke 19:11-27). Luke places these accounts in his canon just prior to Jesus' triumphal entry into Jerusalem, which is Palm Sunday.

For now we focus on Zacchaeus, who serves as any man or woman. He is an archetype, a man who has failed to resist the materialism that is empire, until he met Jesus. "Jesus said, 'Zacchaeus, hurry and come down; for I must stay at your house today.' So he hurried down and was happy to welcome him. All who saw it began to grumble and said, 'He has gone to be the guest of one who is a sinner.'" This small segment is significant. The writer informs readers that those around Zacchaeus did not trust him; in addition; they were aware that Zacchaeus was no longer resistant to empire but fully took advantage of it and supported it. We know this because it is a part of his confession and repentance. Zacchaeus was willing to pay retribution; he was willing to pay economic reparations to those he exploited. "Zacchaeus stood there and said to the Lord, 'Look, half of my possessions, Lord, I will give to the poor; and if I have defrauded anyone of anything, I will pay back four times as much.'" At this point, the writer says that Jesus forgives Zacchaeus for his sins (Luke 19:1-10).

Luke's pattern is similar to that of the passage from Exodus. We see the collective liberation narrative, the human justice movement, and ensuing economic reparations. We notice the presence of the movement when we see Jesus moving with a large crowd that followed him through Jericho. The writer of Luke also permits readers to detect the formation of the collective liberation narrative's focus on unjust material wealth at the expense of oppressed people. We remember that Zacchaeus was "a chief tax collector and was rich." Then, Luke generously offers his readers a thematic pattern: Zacchaeus takes upon himself the responsibility to repent with contrition and confession of his sins. Zacchaeus's sins were personal but required a public remedy. His transgressions involved defrauding the poor; in a fair and just society there are moral and legal remedies, which is economic reparations.

My intent has been to provide a brief but necessary exposition that includes a collective liberation narrative and a human justice movement: how they form and function and lead to economic reparations. In Exodus and in Luke, we notice that Yahweh's justice occurs canonically and syntactically during or near Passover. What is of import here is the collective liberation narrative, the human justice movement, and economic restitution present in Old and New Testament passages. I further believe that reading in this manner will help readers to interpret texts as literary tools that claim Yahweh is the God of justice and liberation.

Now I will trace this aforementioned thematic pattern toward successful modern-era Jewish economic reparations and attempt to understand the failures of people of African descent to receive economic reparations. For now, Passover is a point of departure for the collective liberation narrative and human justice movement, which continues and seeks justice in forms of economic reparations.

In pursuit of successful claims to economic reparations, we may take into consideration those made by Rhoda E. Howard Hassmann and Anthony P. Lombardo.[1] Howard-Hassmann and Lombardo are the authors of "Framing Reparations Claims: Differences Between the African and Jewish Social Movements for Reparations," and their thesis can be summarized in the following way: Success in receiving economic reparations "depends to a large extent on how any claim for reparations is framed."[2] In this chapter I have cited what I consider to be plausible examples from the Hebrew human justice movement (Exodus 12; Luke 19:1-10). Howard-Hassmann and Lombardo see the successes of modern Jewish claims for reparation as a result of telling a good story with a highly organized and functional social movement (human justice movement) that dramatizes their claims. This happens due in part to a carefully crafted message that reinforces the claims made.[3] In short, this means that a reparation claim is presented in a narrow scope and is reinforced by a clear, concise, singular message that is argued consistently in public and private spheres.

People of African descent may adopt a similar strategy. We possess the most identifiable and collective liberation narrative and human justice movement of the twentieth century. That is, we must capitalize and make known well our reparation claim and broadly make it noticed by the larger public. A human (social) movement by definition is something that "frames or assigns meaning to and interprets relevant events and conditions in ways that are intended to mobilize potential adherents and constituents to garner bystander support, and to demobilize antagonists."[4] I agree with Howard-Hassmann and Lombardo: framing our claim requires a collective (liberation) narrative and an organized human (social) movement. But where do we start? We begin by framing that economic reparations are a part of our collective liberation narrative.

The Collective Liberation Narrative of People of African Descent

People of African descent have a shared common experience. By this, I mean that wherever we have placed our feet in the Caribbean, Africa, the Americas, and the Diaspora at large, people of African descent have been subjugated economically and sociopsychologically by the relentless rule of dominating empire. We must then pursue remedy by means of justice motifs which are at the taproot of our collective liberation narrative. Our starting point is to frame and make known that our demand for economic reparations is shared by people of African descent. It is this species we call our collective liberation narrative that informs, shapes, and sharpens our claim for economic reparations. The claim is sharpened and shaped by a widely recognized human justice movement and leaders.

The success of our reparation claim depends on our organizing spokespersons, highly respected persons, who will make our reparation claim internationally. These leaders are best decided early in our organization process. If we consider the Jewish approach, this brief example may be helpful. In "The Early History of German-Jewish Reparations," Menachem Z. Rosensaft and Joana D. Rosensaft retell how early Jewish leaders emerged at the end of their Holocaust:

There exist several detailed accounts of the inception of German-Jewish reparations. However, while the identities and accomplishments of the principal protagonists of the early reparations saga, such as Dr. Nahum Goldman, President of the World Jewish Congress ("WJC") and of the Claims Conference, and Dr. Noah Barou, one of the leaders of the WJC's British section and Chairman of the European Executive of the WJC, are acknowledged. . . .

[Josef] Rosensaft was one of the first, together with Noah Barou, who felt that Germany should not be permitted to keep the untold treasures stolen by the Nazis from Jewish communities throughout Europe, that Germany should be made to pay in some measure for the expense of rehabilitating surviving Jews and restoring to them a measure of their assets. It was these two men who prevailed upon Nahum Goldman to undertake the leadership which resulted in the successful culmination of the effort to recover restitution and reparations from the postwar Federal German Republic.[5]

What is important here is that widely recognized Jewish organizations and leaders emerged and began to shape their human justice movement by reciting their well-known collective liberation narrative. It is certain the Jewish people understood that it was their responsibility to pursue economic reparations. They had been abused morally and ethically by the German empire. However, Jewish people and spheres are conditioned to respond. They had received reparations from Pharaoh, who represents empire (Exodus 14:26-28). Therefore they believed well that they were deserving of reparations from the German empire.

Historically, the Americanized organizations of our people of African descent (leaders of what will be called "spheres") have included the National Council of Negro Women (NCNW), the National Association for the Advancement of Colored People (NAACP), the National Urban League (NUL), the National Association of Black Journalists (NAABJ), and widely recognized ecclesial organizations such as the National Baptist Convention USA, Inc. (NBC USA, Inc.), the Progressive National Baptist Convention, USA, Inc. (PNBC, USA, Inc.), the African Methodist Episcopal Church (AMEC), and other venerable religious bodies. However, our expectations from leaders in these spheres must be modified. Some lack a missional orientation to lead our human justice movement (our liberation march) toward making a successful claim to receive economic reparations.

We must identify, then, leaders who support our international assignment. Our assignment is to present a clear reparation claim to an international body. Many of our traditional leaders in public and private spheres do not have an international reach, recognition, and respect. What is more, we cannot see their leadership on economic reparations; we do not read their academic publications on the subject that expresses their grasp of the grave consequences that await us should we fail. This includes our ecclesial leaders; many do not possess a radicalized international vision. We need visionary leaders who understand that the collective liberation narrative works best in conjunction with a human justice movement. Narrative and movement are necessary to make a successful claim for economic reparations on behalf of people of African descent in international settings and contexts.

Indeed there are economic reparation organizations that have a national and international scope: the National Black United Front and Reparation Movement, the National Coalition of Blacks for Reparations in America (N'COBRA), National African American Reparations Commission (NAARC), Jamaica National Reparations Commission, and Institute of the Black World Twenty-first Century are among the leading organizations that are committed to the human justice movement and capable of providing grassroots direction to the aforementioned national organizations of people of African descent.

In our dogged pursuit of economic reparations, there are academic personalities who inform, shape, and sharpen our collective liberation narrative and human justice movement. Some are Michelle Alexander, author of *The New Jim Crow*; Molefi Kete Asante, fountainhead of Afrocentricity and author of *The Painful Demise of Eurocentrism*; Mary Frances Berry, author of *My Face Is Black Is True*; Allan Aubrey Boesak and Curtiss Paul DeYoung, authors of *Radical Reconciliation: Beyond Political Pietism and Christian Quietism,* who are also advocates for economic reparations for people of African descent globally; and radicalized Christian human and civil rights lawyer Bryan Stevenson, who has written *Just Mercy*.[6] This is our starting point to discover inspired and informed leaders.[7]

It is critical that we locate highly respected leaders in the spheres who are dogged advocates to make our reparations claim globally. These leaders in the spheres must catch the *Zeitgeist* and Spirit-filled headwinds. Moreover, leaders in the spheres must influence grassroots organizations and must be influenced by these grassroots organizations. Grassroots organizations oftentimes capture the current moods and sentiments of radicalized resistors. The aforementioned highly respected organizations can learn from grassroots resistors and harness what is described here as inspired synergy. That is, resistance usually coalesces in response to immoral, unethical, illegal actions taken against a certain mass of people. Without these careful steps, we cannot confront empire.

What has been described thus far becomes circular. On the one hand, we need international spokespersons who are supported by organizations that possess a national and international presence. On the other hand, organizational leaders are responsible to influence and be influenced by radicalized grassroots organizations. We must keep in mind, however, it is the collective liberation narrative that coalesces all parties of interest. What follows is an attempt to demonstrate how the collective liberation narrative becomes flesh through the organized human justice movement.

Our Human Justice Movement Becomes Flesh

Our collective liberation narrative becomes flesh in our human justice movement and then in our claim for economic reparations. The human justice movement dramatically emphasizes our collectiveness as we draw attention to our reparations claim in the spheres. Significant traits are consistent within all human justice movements. For example, we look for people who are inspired, informed, and motivated by a common justice motif. The yearning for justice is shared collectively by nonsectarian and religionists. We know that our organic resistance becomes an authentic human justice movement when it has deliberately and successfully influenced and changed hegemonic inhuman cultural norms and policies. There are three factors that we further make saliently important.

First, the collective liberation narrative justifies our call for reparations. Second, our human justice movement provides flesh to the reparations call in the spheres. The narrative, however, is effective when it is narrow in scope and forms a condensing claim to the spheres. The human justice movement frames the claim; its actors have specific assignments that include dramatizing and emphasizing the claim through our collective liberation narrative, which is receiving economic reparations for historic and current oppressive actions caused by an unrelenting ruling empire.

What is third? We must define economic reparations. Economic reparation is simplified here as justice: "Justice requires not only ceasing and desisting of injustice but also requires either punishment or reparation for injuries and damages inflicted for prior wrongdoing. The essence of injustice is the redistribution of [that] earned through the perpetration of injustice."[8] Reparation claims for people of African descent have an inherent blockade: empire is our opponent.

Empire Is as Old as the Prophet Moses

Empire is a superior nation-state that supremely rules over and cajoles weaker nation-states to comply with rules set forth by the unrivaled power which is empire. It is my view that this points toward the capacity of colonial and postcolonial powers to impose their will upon the nation-states of the African continent. The Accra Confession (2004), however, makes central to its definition that empire remains beyond colonial and postcolonial hegemonic power:

> We speak of empire, because we discern a coming together of economic, cultural, political and military power in our world today. This is constituted by a reality and a spirit of lordless domination, created by humankind. An all-encompassing global reality serving, protecting and defending the interests of powerful corporations, nations, elites and privileged people, while exploiting creation, imperiously excludes, enslaves and even sacrifices humanity. It is a persuasive spirit of destructive self-interest, even greed—the worship of money, goods and possessions; the gospel of consumerism, proclaimed through powerful propaganda and religiously justified, believed and followed. It is the colonization of

consciousness, values and notions of human life by the imperial logic; a spirit of lacking compassionate justice and showing contemptuous disregard for the gifts of creation and the household of life.[9]

Empire is comprehensive. By this I mean empire possesses consolidated power, namely, economic, cultural, political, and military. In addition, empire is a human hegemonic construct that seeks global lordless dominance. Among other things, empire employs strategic forms of manipulation and exploitation that are manifested through consumerism, possessions, and propaganda. Oftentimes empire's power is coalesced through its self-approved justification, erroneous religious claims, and slithering serpent-like imperialism. We see this in Eurocentric cultures.

As was previously mentioned, I contend that Old and New Testament passages demonstrate that a human justice movement and collective liberation narrative are employed to resist empire. For example, we identify this in Mosaic literature. We see a deliberate presentation of heroic figures in the collective liberation narrative that are representative of human agency in the human justice liberation movement.[10] The Mosaic collective liberation narrative guides its readers toward a cultural preunderstanding of an Afrocentric resistance culture.

At a closer reading, we immediately notice the actions of the Hebrew midwives, including Shiphrah and Puah (Exodus 1:15). These courageous women disobeyed the hegemonic edict of empire (Pharaoh). They made a moral and ethical decision not to obey a hegemonic–demonic expectation to murder innocent children. These heroic women refused to destroy the lives of their African sons. In the collective liberation narrative, we witness other courageous actors emerge as resistant to empire. Jochebed is Moses' biological mother; Miriam is Moses' biological sister, Pharaoh's daughter is Moses' surrogate mother, and Zipporah is Moses' wife (Exodus 2:1-10; 4:24-26; 6:20).

Like the midwives before them, these women are significant heroic figures in Exodus and in the collective liberation narrative and human justice movement. Pharaoh's daughter remains nameless, but a daughter of Pharaoh named Bithiah may be our courageous heroine (see 1 Chronicles 4:18). We must be careful that we do not devalue these who are shaping the Hebrew collective liberation narrative and who are leading this human justice movement. We find this notion of devaluation similar to what bell hooks describes as the "Integrity of Black Womanhood":

> Black women active in the struggle for black liberation and all social movements advocating women's rights both in the past and in the present have continually resisted this devaluation. Our resistance has intensified as we have struggled to place transforming cultural attitudes about the representation of black women on the agendas of both the black liberation movement and the contemporary feminist movement.[11]

It is important that we not lose sight that the women of the collective liberation narrative and human justice movement in Exodus are African woman of integrity who serve as our contemporary archetypes. By that, I mean they are people who serve as symbols of an egalitarian resistance struggle. What is more, their human justice resistance occurs simultaneously with an emerging collective liberation narrative.

When Yahweh commands the people of Hebrew descent to depart Egypt, which is empire, their oppressors provided economic reparations (Exodus 12:33-36). Although the role of the heroines of Exodus is presented subtly and with nuance, the Mosaic writer is clear. The heroines of Exodus are signifiers. That is, the actions of these courageous women represent an emerging collective liberation narrative and human justice movement for people of African descent.

It is clear that the Passover is more than atonement for personal sins; it is too a human justice movement complemented by a collective liberation narrative (Exodus 12). The narrative and the movement demanded and received economic reparations from people who benefitted from empire. The struggles that we see in Exodus mirror and inform our current liberation struggle. I contend that the collective liberation narrative and human justice movement in Exodus are a point of departure for our collective liberation narrative and human justice movement.

There are other factors that we must consider, and none are more important than the Du Boisian construct of race, economics, and politics.[12] It is certain Du Bois's construct shapes our collective liberation narrative, human justice narrative, and global positioning system (GPS) toward economic reparations. This matters, because unlike the Jewish community, we have not gained support from the United States and the international European community for our reparations claim. We have not been able to jump high enough or through obviously racially biased proverbial hoops.[13]

We must keep in mind, however, that Howard-Hassmann's and Lombardo's critique suggests that the reparation claim of people of African descent is hindered because of a lack of coordination. In their view, we have not utilized our collective liberation narrative and human justice movement in an organized effort to make our reparations claim successfully. Also, we have not formed a sustainable strategy that we have assigned to our human justice movement that explains our demands to the masses and our struggle against empire. Our largest opponent, however, is not our lack of effort but empire.

We point directly toward empire as the historic oppressor of people of African descent. It is this current and toxic order that continues to neglect the obvious: we have been injured and continue to experience irreparable damages to our personhood, psychology, and properties. Our focus then is to tell this story through our collective liberation narrative that informs our human justice movement. Together they provide rhetorical space to make our claim for economic reparations. In general, this claim is to abolish income and wealth inequalities, and specifically we doggedly pursue economic reparations as that remedy.[14] Howard-Hassmann and Lombardo assert that our efforts have been unsuccessful in part because of the lack of a singular and narrow focus.

For contrast and comparison, I include two different ideas about achieving economic reparations for people of African descent. The first is that of Howard-Hassmann and Lombardo. Their view is that people of African descent must organize the claim for economic reparations around a carefully crafted message that comes out of the historic collective liberation narrative and human justice movement. The second is that of Wyatt Tee Walker, a civil rights icon. Walker pointed toward three different ethnic groups—Native Americans, Japanese Americans, and Jewish Americans—who have received economic reparations from the government of the United States in the twentieth and twenty-first centuries.

Howard-Hassmann and Lombardo:

In comparison to the reparations claims of Jewish victims of the Holocaust, then, African claims seem burdened with both substantive and organizational difficulties. At the substantive level, it is difficult to frame a convincing call for reparations because many of the victims are long dead, there are too many of them, and they cannot be easily identified. It is also difficult to identify the perpetrators and the exact injuries they caused. Second, the causal chain between past harms and present victims is long and complex, with many actors and events involved. By contrast, reparation for the Holocaust was easily framed. Both victims and perpetrators were easily identifiable, and the event took place over a short, finite period. The harm was clear, and the causal chain was short and lacking in complexity.[15]

Wyatt Tee Walker:

Now that Barack Obama has been elected as the first black president of the United States, he should seriously consider reparations for African-Americans. The issue has generated a lot of critical commentary from white and black pundits, some worrying that reparations would further erode race relations in the United States. The idea of reparations, however, is non-negotiable. Jews received reparations for their Holocaust. Native Americans received reparations for their genocide at the hands of Europeans. Japanese Americans received reparations for their treatment during World War II. Slavery for African-Americans is our Holocaust, yet we have not received restitution.[16]

Of course we are not treated the same. We cannot follow the exact actions taken by Jewish, Japanese, and Native American communities. Indeed we continue to endure hostile Eurocentric biases collectively and globally. We cannot follow a neat line toward our human liberation through the "good will and means" of the Western institutional spheres. At all cost, these spheres defend Eurocentrism and its Eurocentric narrative, a narrative that inherently denies that it culturally reinforces discrimination against people of African descent. The adherents of Eurocentrism have made it clear that people of African descent will not be considered as others in matters of economic reparations.

Howard-Hassmann and Lombardo, by way of comparison between Jewish reparation successes and African reparation failures, believe that people of African descent have been ineffective in successfully framing our claim. Howard-Hassmann and Lombardo suggest that Jewish economic reparation claims include proverbial dots that are connected by what the authors call a "causal chain."[17] What is more, they suggest that Jewish reparation arguments and appeals are persuasive because "the harm was clear, and the causal chain was short and lacking in complexity."[18] By comparison, Walker believed that "slavery for the African-American is our Holocaust."[19] This is the frame, and an effective causal chain. Walker talked about the continuing ramifications of slavery that were evident in the entire twentieth century and continuing into the twenty-first century. Walker rightly pointed out that empire has conceded moral and legal culpability for Native, Japanese, and Jewish Americans' injustices. Rightly, these citizens have received reparations. Along those same lines, people of African descent in America should receive similar restitution in forms of economic reparations.

Therefore, what has been inferred is that reparation claims for people of African descent are not narrow in scope, and we do not share our common and collective liberation narrative; we do not shape and sharpen our similar message; we do not develop our universal organizational objectives and goals; we do not have an organized, universal human justice movement that is both inspired and informed to compel empire to make awarding policy changes. Successful outcomes here are to change hegemonic norms that are the seedbed for unfair and unequal economic reparation policies. In short, what matters is framing. Our argument and appeal are to make specific reparations claims, against specific perpetrators, in a specific time and place, and against specific people in that time and space. What we have described here is our narrow path.

Conclusion

What is meant by path is our common pathology, which is a characteristic trait present in a narrative development, but here path and pathology are narrowed to what Howard-Hassmann and Lombardo call a "causal chain."[20] The chain connects the dots "between the harmful action and a claim for reparations."[21] As indicated, a successful narrative that leads to economic reparations is narrow in focus, and therefore the scope is clear. It points to specific times and places that involve injured people and the people who have caused those injuries, whether living or dead.

This is a common characterization associated with a so-called causal chain. Who are the victims? Who caused the victimization? Where did these events occur? When did these events occur? Why did these events occur? How did these events occur? What we do know? Currently these questions are neither asked nor answered adequately by the dominating classes and culture. These questions and answers are not addressed, nevertheless; these are a ghastly part of the Eurocentric narrative. Therefore, a new or different narrative must emerge to ask and answer these questions. The Eurocentric narrative lacks moral courage to lead on this seminally critical demand for human justice. The collective liberation narrative of people of African descent, however, must lead, be informed, and be reinforced by an ongoing simultaneous and associated human justice movement. "Any successful social [human justice] movement also requires a compelling framing of its demand for change. This applies just as much to the demand for reparations for an injustice as to any other demand, however moral and self-evident the demand may seem to those making it."[22]

We define a successful human justice movement by evidence that points toward its impact upon moral and legal changes in public and private spheres. Human justice movements are the seedbed for social theory, and this theoretical point of departure influences moral, ethical, and legal policies. Without policies, we know that change will not occur and will not endure. Said another way, we need human justice movements that dramatize our collective liberation narrative. We need a collective liberation narrative that provides a clearly defined and substantiated psychospiritual and philosophical collective liberation theory that insists that our human justice movement resist empire while at the same time it supports our dogged pursuit of moral, ethical, and legal claims for economic reparations which epitomizes our human rights. Here, human rights are narrowed to the dogged pursuit to achieve income and wealth equalities by people of African descent. By way of synthesis, this points toward economic reparations.

Next the movement enlists advocates for what we universally claim. All resisting advocates must be inspired, impassioned, and informed by our counterhegemonic narrative. It is the narrative that is our point of departure; it frames our argument and claim for economic reparations. The collective liberation narrative continues to grow and reshape itself out of the activism chronicled in the ongoing human justice movement. The human justice activists are grassroots heroes and heroines like the Hebrew midwives Shiphrah and Puah; Jochebed, Moses' biological mother; Miriam, Moses' biological sister; Pharaoh's daughter, Moses' surrogate mother; and Zipporah, Moses' wife (Exodus 1:15; 2:1-10; 4:24-26; 6:20).

We must work between theory and practical application. Theory is located in our collective liberation narrative, and practical application is located in our human justice movement. Together these result in economic reparations. This is a clear roadmap, but it needs cultivation among well-informed participants, dedicated people who will agree to focus on specific strategies that are communicated clearly for implementation. In this way, we are an inspired and impassioned people who understand our valuable roles and precise actions against oppressors and state-sanctioned regimes.

We have claimed that economic reparations function in Old and New Testament collective liberation narratives and human justice movements. For this chapter, I focused narrowly on Exodus 12 and Luke 19:1-10. Furthermore, I observed that a thematic pattern emerged that includes a collective liberation narrative and a human justice movement that result in economic restitution. I believe this balance between theory and practical application informs strategies for Jewish economic reparations. We are not Jewish, and we are not treated as such, but we are morally and ethically responsible to analyze their approach because we trace that approach to Scripture. We love Yahweh's justice, and we love our people.

NOTES

1. Rhoda E. Howard-Hassmann and Anthony P. Lombardo, "Framing Reparations Claims: Differences Between the African and Jewish Social Movements for Reparations," *African Studies Review* 50, no. 1 (April 2007): 27–48.
2. Ibid., 27.
3. Ibid.

4. Ibid., 28.

5. Menachem Z. Rosensaft and Joana D. Rosensaft, "The Early History of German-Jewish Reparations," *Fordham International Law Journal* 25, issue 6, article 2 (2001): 4–5.

6. See Michelle Alexander, *The New Jim Crow: Mass Incarceration in the Age of Colorblindness* (New York: The New Press, 2010); Molefi Kete Asante, *The Painful Demise of Eurocentrism: An Afrocentric Response to Critics* (Trenton, NJ: Africa World Press, 1999); Mary Frances Berry, *My Face Is Black Is True: Callie House and the Struggle for Ex-Slave Reparations* (New York: Alfred A. Knopf, 2005); Allan Aubrey Boesak and Curtiss Paul DeYoung, *Radical Reconciliation: Beyond Political Pietism and Christian Quietism* (Maryknoll, NY: Orbis Books, 2016); Bryan Stevenson, *Just Mercy: A Story of Justice and Redemption* (New York: Spiegel and Grau, 2014).

7. See Raymond A. Winbush, ed., *Should America Pay? Slavery and the Raging Debate on Reparations* (New York: Amistad, 2003).

8. Amos N. Wilson, *Blueprint for Black Power: A Moral, Political, and Economic Imperative for the Twenty-First Century* (New York: Afrikan World InfoSystems, 1998), 459.

9. Allan Aubrey Boesak, *Dare We Speak of Hope? Searching for a Language of Life in Faith and Politics* (Grand Rapids: Eerdmans, 2014), 55–56.

10. Joseph Evans, *Lifting the Veil over Eurocentrism: The Du Boisian Hermeneutic of Double Consciousness* (Trenton, NJ: Africa World Press, 2014), 156. See the Du Boisian folk and mythical hero rhetorical strategy and consider it a similar and parallel rhetorical strategy to develop a collective liberation narrative that is present in Old and New Testament texts.

11. bell hooks, *killing rage: Ending Racism* (New York: Henry Holt and Company, 1995), 78.

12. W. E. B. Du Bois, *Dusk of Dawn: An Essay Toward an Autobiography of a Race Concept* (Piscataway, NJ: Transactions Publishers, 2011), 47.

13. Hilary Beckles, *Britain's Black Debt: Reparations for Caribbean Slavery and Native Genocide* (Barbados: University of The West Indies Press, 2013), 176. Beckles writes, "The United States had already declared non-participation in objection of the word 'reparation' appearing on the draft agenda [Durban Conference on reparations, 2007]. The European Union and 'Western' countries threatened to remove themselves for the same reason. Colin Powell, [then] the secretary of [US] state, and Condoleezza Rice, national security advisor, both African Americans, were bullish about the matter, stating that the world must not tell the United States how to handle its racial past and present." See also "Rice Says US Blacks Should Not Be Paid for Slavery," *Daily Observer*, September 10, 2001.

14. See Thomas Piketty, *Capital in the Twenty-First Century* (Cambridge, MA: The Belknap Press of Harvard University Press, 2014). "The distribution of wealth is one of today's most widely discussed and controversial issues," 1.

15. Howard-Hassmann and Lombardo, "Framing Reparations Claims," 32.

16. Wyatt Tee Walker, "Case for Reparations," *Style Weekly* (November 26, 2008), http://m.styleweekly.com/richmond/the-case-for-reparations/Content?oid=1363042, accessed May 6, 2017.

17. Howard-Hassmann and Lombardo, "Framing Reparations Claims," 32.

18. Ibid.

19. Walker, "Case for Reparations."

20. Howard-Hassmann and Lombardo, "Framing Reparations Claims," 32.

21. Ibid.

22. Ibid., 28.

CHAPTER 6

Fallible Humanity

The Double Consciousness
of Thomas Jefferson

The history of the University of Virginia is, like the larger history of the United States, the story of Thomas Jefferson's vision and of how that vision grew into the lively, democratic place we know today. Mr. Jefferson believed that education was essential to the new republic—an education available universally, not just to those who could afford it. Nearly two hundred years later, within the walls of his academic village, men and women of all backgrounds debate—and often criticize—the ideas of their university's founder, perhaps the best testimony of all to the spirit and success of his vision.[1]
—Susan Tyler Hitchcock

I was amazed at the proximity between the classes and races of bodily remains that lie at rest in the University of Virginia cemetery. I entered from the south side and immediately was confronted by a tall stone figure, an image of a Confederate soldier. The stone's inscription read "Confederate Dead." The monument is a reminder of the Civil War and a commemoration of those who died for their failed southern cause. I gazed toward the monument through a glaring midday sun, and it occurred to me that I was standing among graves of people who had dedicated themselves to their proposition that all people were not created as equals. It came to my mind that these fallen Confederate soldiers fought to keep my ancestors as slaves indefinitely. I have never felt claustrophobic before, but I was emotionally transported into another historical period. It was like standing in the Valley of Dry Bones (Ezekiel 37:1-14). If these bones lived again, would they remain ardently against civil and human rights? The United States Civil War was their failed cause. It was not over states' rights. Instead, their cause was about who determined what constitutes human equality.

I moved forward but with an eerie feeling. Still, I moved forward with courage, maybe as my ancestors did, with an imaginary Ghanaian drum master's beat that kept my pace deliberate. As I walked over the manicured grass, I did not escape the bright sun gleams that created a prism of light. The prism's streams pierced the cemetery and cast deep shadows into parts of the space that made it difficult for me to read some of the names on the headstones that were proximate to me. Still, I managed to glance at some of them. I did not stop to admire. I did not stop to muse or adjure. The dead could not hear or answer me. Instead, I read some of their names, such as Taylor, Egger, Beams, and Gooch. I was determined to remember their humanity.

Then I looked to the west and made sure that I had kept my bearing and directional orientation. I glanced to the east, where I knew that space was dedicated to the memory of many of the university's prominent alumni, academicians, and former presidents whose remains lie in state and rest. Though I am not an expert on the quality of headstones, those in the east appeared to be made of a fairer cut and a higher quality than those of their Confederate dead. Although these lie in proximity, it was obvious that the cemetery was segregated not only by racial distinctions but also by class among the southern and Confederate dead.

I did not make the journey to Charlottesville to make these observations. I had come to witness the burial sites of the sixty-seven.

I came to see the space that is just outside the university cemetery's northern gate. The space that I came to see is where sixty-seven slaves unknown by their proper names are buried. This third class of people, people of African descent, did not have monuments or headstones, not even markers. It was as though they did not matter; it was as though they were not human.

It was in 2012 that the graves of the sixty-seven were discovered during an archaeological excavation:

On Oct. 22, 2012, a University of Virginia landscaping crew began clearing topsoil from land just north of the University Cemetery. Founded in 1828, the cemetery provides a final resting place for University presidents, faculty members, prominent alumni and even a Civil War general. Now a planned expansion of the cemetery had the crew, under the supervision of local archeologists, taking a peek under a thick, two-foot-deep layer of dirt that covered a former plant nursery. An earlier survey had turned up nothing, but this time the archeologists spotted a subtle change in the soil's color and texture, forming what became, after a bit more digging, an unmistakable pattern. Laid out before them, an irregular check board stamped in the red Virginia clay, was a series of poorly marked and unmarked grave shafts, 67 in all.[2]

One of the archaeologists in charge of the dig made the following statement: "The significant number of grave shafts identified in the burial ground suggest the use by a large population associated with the University. . . . With the exception of students, the largest population of individuals living on Grounds at the University [at the time the graves were believed to be filled] would have been enslaved African Americans."[3] Like the academicians, alumni, presidents, and Confederate dead, the sixty-seven now have manicured grass and markers on the west and south sides that commemorate their lives.

What is of equal import is that this is the cemetery of Mr. Jefferson's university. He is not interred there; his remains are at Monticello. His headstone (monument) reads:

> Here was buried
> Thomas Jefferson
> Author of the Declaration of American Independence
> Of the Statute of Virginia for religious freedom
> And Father of the University of Virginia[4]

One reason I have chosen to tell this story of Jefferson is to bring attention to his humanity; Jefferson demonstrated throughout his life that he functioned with double consciousness and other human contradictions. I hope to compel readers to listen with open minds and hearts to our need to bring healing to the millions of people of African descent who have lived their lives within the veil. The account builds a bridge to the previous chapter, where I described a collective liberation narrative and human justice movement.

The story that I have told is also an accurate reappraisal of events that make Thomas Jefferson and his university the subject of what the ministry of reconciliation could look like in real time and space—in short, what the ministry of reconciliation can look like in application. Therefore, this chapter serves as a bridge to the next chapter, for when our collective liberation narrative and human justice movement are nearly the same—that is, in messaging, strategy, and tactics—we see human equality. I see human equality in terms of economic justice, which is economic reparations.

Jefferson's Intellectual and Emotional Contradictions

I begin my characterization of Thomas Jefferson by trying to understand his intellectual and emotional contradictions, something that I describe as his double consciousness. I contend that it is consistent with W. E. B. Du Bois's definition thereof. Furthermore, I contend that Jefferson's double consciousness surfaces, in part, due to his interactions with Parisian and European claims of cultural superiority compared with American culture. Second, Jefferson's intellectual and emotional contradictions are noticed in his relationship with his slaves, particularly Sally Hemings.

Jefferson's Relationship with His Slaves

Thomas Jefferson, the intellectual architect of the Declaration of Independence and the third president of the United States, was born on April 17, 1743, on Shadwell Plantation near Charlottesville, Virginia. He died at his Monticello ("little mountain") plantation that overlooks the Shadwell and Charlottesville, on July 4, 1826. At his death, Jefferson is said to have spoken his last words to his attending physician, Robley Dunglison; his grandson, Thomas Jefferson Randolph; and Nicholas Trist, the husband of Virginia Randolph Trist, Jefferson's granddaughter.[5] All remembered the occasion, but not in the same way.

All agreed that Jefferson was concerned with the Fourth of July.[6] This is understandable; Jefferson knew well that the date, that is, the Fourth of July, had symbolic meaning. It was the symbolic birthday of perhaps the greatest nation and democracy in the history of the world. It also chronicled his life's work and memorialized his dedication to forming the nation's ethos, pathos, and no less its mythologies. Jefferson, however, did speak to other people: "At 4 a.m. on the 4th, Jefferson did speak again. Randolph writes that Jefferson called in the servants 'with a strong and clear voice.' But what he actually said to them, Randolph unfortunately does not reveal. Jefferson lingered until 12:50 in the afternoon, but Randolph is clear that his last words were spoken that morning to the servants."[7]

"Servants" was a kind and genteel way for Jefferson to describe his slaves. In an 1898 *Alumni Bulletin* of the University of Virginia, the term *servants* reemerges. Ben Ford, the supervisor of the archaeological dig that was previously mentioned, "points to a clue found in an 1898 *Alumni Bulletin,* in which the son of a former University librarian referred to 'servants,' a common euphemism for 'slaves,' in his recollection that 'in old times, the University servants were buried on the north side of the cemetery, just outside of the wall.'"[8]

C. C. Wertenbaker, the son of that former university librarian, responded to an inquiry about the history of the university cemetery. He claimed that the first body was laid to rest there in 1828, and in ensuing years many others were interred there. As part of his recollection, Wertenbaker made the following statements: "In the old times, the University servants were buried on the north side of the cemetery just outside of the wall, but it was then said that many bodies were only logs of wood or stones for fear of having their dead taken up by the medical class (then entirely dependent on their own enterprise for subjects), [which] caused the negroes to inter their dead secretly, and hold the usual ceremonies over the dummy."[9]

Notice that Wertenbaker employs the Jeffersonian term *servants*, though the sixty-seven indeed were slaves. We sense Jefferson's influence upon the university's culture seventy-two years after his death; he was the father of the university. This terminology further illuminates southern culture, its politeness or even polity. To call the sixty-seven servants instead of slaves had become an unwritten rule (polity). "Servants" was a way to speak in language that pointed toward the Jeffersonian lexicon. It is a deliberate refusal, however, to reckon with what had happened in the American south. Wertenbaker speaks of the deceased as less than human, suggesting that some of their bodies were not interred in the university cemetery. Instead, "only logs of wood or stone" were buried for fear that medical students would exhume their bodies and use them as experimental cadavers.

Nevertheless, the people who Jefferson needed were at his bedside—his slaves.[10] Who were these slaves, and why were they summoned there during the time that he escaped his mortal flesh? What is the connection between Jefferson's life, death, and his slaves? In his final words, did Jefferson speak well? Did he speak words of thanksgiving and charity? Did Jefferson offer to his slaves words of pardon or paradox? As a part of his benediction, did Jefferson speak to his slaves a word of reconciliation?

Whether Jefferson did so or not is merely my speculation. However, we do know that Burwell Colbert and Sally Hemings were two of Jefferson's slaves at his side near the end of his life. We know that another slave, Wormley Hughes, dug Jefferson's grave:

> As Jefferson faded his grandson Jeff Randolph and the others remembered, "He [Jefferson] would only have his servants sleep near him." Randolph makes clear that more than one enslaved person was deeply involved with Jefferson's care in his final days. That is not surprising. There were more than enough Hemingses to stand watch, and in those intense moments the attention of the entire place was riveted by the man who for over five decades had dominated the consciousness, imaginations, and lives of everyone who lived on the mountain. Randolph did not name all of the "servants" who attended Jefferson, but it is almost certain that they included, at the very least, Burwell Colbert and Sally Hemings, the only two people said to have taken care of his rooms and him. As is often the case with those on their deathbeds, Jefferson had trouble sleeping, and people took turns sitting up with him during the day and at night. He did not want to be alone, and insisted that his enslaved caregivers make pallets so they could sleep in the room with him overnight. Only they were allowed in his bedroom after dark, and anxious members of the Randolph family took to making secret forays into his bedchamber to check on their loved one.[11]

We too know that John Hemings "crafted" Jefferson's wooden casket and that Jefferson was interred in the Monticello family cemetery with Martha and Maria.[12] Martha Wayles Skelton Jefferson, Jefferson's wife, died on September 6, 1782. She did not live to see her husband serve as the third president of the United States (1801–1809). Maria Jefferson Eppes, Jefferson's daughter, died due to complications of her pregnancy at Monticello in April 1804. "Watching from afar, Jefferson suggested that Maria might be better off at the more well-appointed Monticello. Determining that a carriage ride would tax her too much, enslaved men made a litter and carried the young mother up the hill [from her sister's home, the Edgehill] to the place of her birth."[13]

At the time of his own death, we know that Jefferson manumitted five slaves: Burwell Colbert, Joseph Fossett, and Eston, John, and Madison Hemings. However, we also know that he did not make legal and binding arrangements to manumit Sally Hemings. Why? Some have said that he did not because he sought to protect his own legacy and reputation. Always Jefferson was the master strategist and tactician. Although he drifted in and out of consciousness, Jefferson was aware of how he wanted to be remembered, and to his dying breath, he sought to protect his reputation and legacy. Whether his protection included his white family's social welfare is unclear to me. He left them in financial debt and ruins for generations. But it is clear, Jefferson had a sociopolitical dilemma that involved Sally Hemings. Her manumission would be a legal issue, particularly if she should choose to remain in Virginia (which she did eventually).

Had Jefferson freed Hemings in his final will and testament, her freedom would have required an affirmative vote from the Virginia legislature. Jefferson's political enemies would have destroyed his legacy and reputation along with his white family's dignity. Beyond hearsay, all would have come to believe and know that Jefferson was the father of mulatto children by Sally Hemings.[14] She was a political object, unfortunately. Hemings's and Jefferson's sexual relation was considered amalgamation.[15]

Jefferson was a master of political calculus. His mastery is noted during his tenure in Paris. In retrospect, Jefferson's political craftiness is obvious when we reconsider his public stance on people of African descent. Jefferson argued that compared with whites, blacks were inferior. After a careful study of Jefferson's cultural context, his public rhetoric, and his private affairs, I characterize his intellectual and emotional contradictions to be motivated by political expediency. Jefferson tapped into the *Zeitgeist*, which was a hyper-Eurocentric elitism; this was both intellectual and emotional for Jefferson. To be a political racist was chic then, and it is now. Jefferson was no different from George Wallace, the segregationist governor of Alabama in the 1960s, who uttered these infamous words: "Today I have stood, where once Jefferson Davis stood, and took an oath to my people. . . . In the name of the greatest people that have ever trod this earth, I draw the line in the dust and toss the gauntlet before the feet of tyranny . . . and I say . . . segregation today . . . segregation tomorrow . . . segregation forever."[16]

Jefferson's *Notes on the State of Virginia* reflects this sentiment. I consider *Notes* to be an early portal into the political and religious mind of Jefferson. I also consider it to be an early portal into Jefferson's double consciousness, which indicates his intellectual and emotional contradictions.

A definition for double consciousness is paramount for understanding Jefferson and his white southern acrimony. For this definition, we turn to Du Bois:

> It is a peculiar sensation, this double-consciousness, this sense of always looking at one's self through the eyes of others, of measuring one's soul by the tape of a world that looks on in amused contempt and pity. One ever feels his twoness,—an American . . . two souls, two thoughts, two unreconciled strivings; two warring ideals in one . . . body, whose dogged strength alone keeps it from being torn asunder.[17]

Du Bois's definition was written to express the social, psychological, and spiritual location of the so-called Negro. However, had Jefferson lived to read it, he would have recognized himself in Du Bois's definition of double consciousness. Du Bois had defined Jefferson's intellectual and emotional contradictions which are a part of double consciousness.

The Powerless Against the Powerful

I believe that we have located double consciousness in the person of Jefferson. At the heart of my assertion, I point toward European intellectual bigotry. That is, compared with European culture, American culture was inferior. Jefferson "quickly discovered that Europeans were superior to Americans in matters of art, music, architecture, science, technology, and cuisine. He even concluded that Europeans were more polite than his countrymen."[18] For Jefferson, this criticism pointed not only to American culture at large but also directly to Virginia's culture and mores. Virginia symbolized and epitomized what the white South thought and believed about itself. Jefferson then must have felt double consciousness. A feeling of inferiority threatens human identity and leads to an insecure and duplicitous pathology.

If Jefferson felt that he and other Virginians were not equal to their European forebears, this means that Jefferson felt that he (and his fellow citizens) was less human. If this peculiar sensation is not refuted immediately, it becomes a description of the powerful against the powerless. The powerful can construct a false narrative about the powerless that becomes a tawdry mythology. Readers will recognize that such a stigma may threaten the humanity of powerless people. This peculiar sensation becomes a species of a pathological psychosis, something that Du Bois describes to be a lack of true self-consciousness. In *The Souls of Black Folk*, Du Bois illustrates this sensation: "After the Egyptian and Indian, the Greek and Roman, the Teuton and Mongolian, the Negro is a sort of seventh son, born with a veil, and gifted with second-sight in this American world,—a world that yields him no true self-consciousness."[19]

In our American socio-academic context, Du Bois's definition has been canonized as the most accurate description of what it means to be powerless against the powerful. This peculiar sensation is nominally thought of as the point of departure for understanding relations and the narrative differences between black and white folks. The powerful is the subject always and the powerless is the object always. We can locate this construct in Jefferson's context in Paris; the Parisians are the subject and Jefferson is the object. In Jefferson's time, this construct can be thought of as New England against Virginia. It is said, "Jefferson envied many things about New England. In the empire of this stalwart Virginian imagination, the perfect republican society looked a great deal like New England, and almost nothing like Virginia."[20]

In this instance, the construct of the powerful and the powerless is an intramural scrimmage among the dominating classes and cultural context of people of European descent. What is at stake here is to provide plausibility that Jefferson felt inferior to his European forebears and what surfaced was his double consciousness. In this way, we can make an attempt to get behind Jefferson's inner feelings and motivations which may have compelled him to write *Notes*. It is strongly suggested that the rising awareness of Phillis Wheatley's intellectual poetry surfaced Jefferson's double consciousness. Wheatley's prowess makes us aware of Jefferson's intellectual and emotional contradictions: "To account for this apparent refutation of his inferiority argument, he [Jefferson] redefined [the] poetry [of Phillis Wheatley], insisting that a poem had to be about love—a definition that would exclude a large portion of the world's literature. He declared that Wheatley, who seems to have enraged him, could not be a poet because she wrote about religion."[21]

According to Henry Wiencek, "Jefferson wrote *Notes* as a defense against allegations of American inferiority. He took up the task and pursued it despite so many difficulties and distractions because in his view some French intellectuals had slighted and slandered the New World [and Virginia]."[22] I add that Jefferson was deeply concerned about people of African descent in America's advancement as represented in Wheatley's poetry. Dr. Samuel Johnson, a towering British intellectual, considered Jefferson's claims unsubstantiated, untenable, and hypocritical: "How is it that we hear the loudest yelps for liberty among the drivers of [N]egroes?"[23] Wiencek indirectly reinforces my assertion that European intellectual criticism caused Jefferson to be insecure and vulnerable; quite possibly Jefferson felt less human, and thus he experienced Du Boisian double consciousness.

I have no doubt that Jefferson experienced a deep sense of inferiority to his European intellectual peers. Jefferson, an American southerner, came to Paris with a social stigma and more than likely was reminded of his social inferiority often by his interrogators.[24] The young American in Paris held an intellectual position that was inconsistent with his private emotion. On the one hand, Jefferson had not found a comfortable place to stand on the organic and native genius of Wheatley. On the other hand, Jefferson's private actions that involved Sally Hemings and Burwell Colbert make my argument plausible that Jefferson functioned with double consciousness. Emotionally Jefferson was dependent on his slaves, people he called his "servants."[25]

Enlightenment Attitudes about People of African Descent

In part, *Notes* was Jefferson's refutation against the humanity of people of African descent. Wheatley was the catalyst. Henry Wiencek observes: "One of Wheatley's most famous works not only undermines Jefferson's contention that blacks could not write but also stood as proof of African American loyalty to the American cause."[26] Gates points out that Jefferson was a reactionary and that he spoke in unison with other notable racist intellectuals of his day. Gates writes that Jefferson "argued that blacks were 'imitative' rather than 'creative'. All along, however, black people were merely Signifyin(g) through a motivated repetition."[27] Gates continues:

> So widespread was the debate over "the nature of the African" between 1730 and 1830 that not until the Harlem Renaissance would the work of black writers be as extensively reviewed as it was in the eighteenth century. Phillis Wheatley's list of reviewers included Voltaire, Thomas Jefferson, George Washington, Samuel Rush and James Beatty, to list only a few. Francis Williams's work was analyzed by no less than David Hume and Immanuel Kant. [Georg] Hegel, writing in the *Philosophy of History* in 1813, used the absence of writing of Africans as the sign of their innate inferiority. The list of commentators is extensive, amounting to a "Who's Who" of the French, English, and American Enlightenment.[28]

Like Gates, Cornel West rightly characterized Jefferson as an intellectual and an institutional racist, as well as an uninformed bigot. West makes a case that Eurocentric intellectualism is grounded in white supremacy. What is more, Jefferson among his intellectual peers reinforced and justified these mythologies. Paradoxically, Eurocentric mythologies are self-perpetuating. On the one hand, mythologies were created to reinforce white supremacy. On the other hand, Eurocentric mythologies perpetuate people who no longer realize that white supremacy is a mythology:

> The intellectual legitimacy of the idea of white supremacy, though is grounded in what we now consider marginal disciplines (especially in its second stage), was pervasive. This legitimacy can be illustrated by the extent to which racism permeated the writings of the major figures

of the Enlightenment. It is important to note that the idea of white supremacy not only was accepted by these figures, but, more important, it was accepted by them *without their having to put forward their own arguments to justify it*. Montesquieu and Voltaire . . . Hume and Jefferson of the Scotch and the American Enlightenment, and Kant . . . not merely held racist views; they also uncritically—during this age of criticism—believed that the *authority* for these views rested in the domain of naturalists, anthropologists, physiognomists and phrenologists.[29]

James Baldwin's *Notes of a Native Son* may be characterized as a kind of satire and lampoon, if not an apologetic defense of his own queer humanity. What is certain, Baldwin's *Notes* impedes Jefferson's hegemonic inequality claims against people of African descent. Like Jefferson, who wrote about his native state of Virginia from Paris, Baldwin was a native son of America who fled to Paris where he wrote about Jeffersonian-American mythologies that perpetuate racism. In fact, Baldwin was familiar with Jefferson's whereabouts two centuries earlier in the St. Germain district and what is now called the Rue Bonaparte.[30]

What follows is a passage that appears in Jefferson's *Notes on the State of Virginia*. The second passage was written by Annette Gordon-Reed, the author of *The Hemingses of Monticello*. My purpose here is to emphasize Jefferson's double consciousness and his intellectual and emotional contradictions. I ask readers to understand that Gordon-Reed is commenting on Jefferson's assertions that people of African descent lack cognitive skills that lead to mastering certain levels of responsibilities in a republican social order.

Jefferson wrote,

The circumstance of superior beauty, is thought worthy attention in the propagation of our horses, dogs, and other domestic animals; why not in that of man? Besides those of colour, figure, and hair, there are other physical distinctions proving a difference of race. They have less hair on the face and body. They secrete less by the kidnies, and more by the glands of the skin, which gives them a very strong and disagreeable odour. . . . Comparing them by their faculties of memory, reason, and imagination, it appears to me, that in memory they are equal to the whites; in reason much inferior, as I think one could scarcely be found capable of tracing and comprehending the investigations of Euclid; and that in imagination they are dull, tasteless, and anomalous . . . It will be right to make great allowances for difference of condition, of education, of conversation, of the sphere in which they move.[31]

Gordon-Reed writes,

George Granger Sr. [a dark-skinned slave] was a paid overseer at Monticello, the only black person ever to hold that position on any of Jefferson's farms. Indeed, Jefferson may have freed him informally before he died. His son George Jr. was the foreman at the nail factory, an operation that Jefferson viewed as critical to his family's finances in the late 1790s and early 1800s. Neither man would have been in his important position had Jefferson truly believed that no blacks could reason above telling a simple story, or that they had to have an infusion of white blood to be basically intelligent.[32]

During the time in which Jefferson was in Paris, he would not allow his slaves George Granger and Ursula Granger to be away from Monticello. They earned the nicknames "Queen and King." Jefferson had "exempted them, along with Elizabeth Hemings, from being hired out."[33] To reinforce Reed's claims, Jefferson's rhetoric is highly contradictory and implausible in that he both intellectually and emotionally believed what he had written in *Notes*. It should be emphasized here that, like West, I assert that Jefferson knew European elites thought of themselves as the superior race, and this racist worldview was consistent with Virginia's race mythologies. Still, his upbringing and his attraction to Sally Hemings raises a red flag about Jefferson's mindset, which I contend points toward his double consciousness and his intellectual and emotional contradictions.

Jefferson as Fallibly Human

I compare Jefferson with Winton Churchill's description of Russia: "a riddle wrapped in a mystery, inside an enigma." Jefferson is an example of what it means to be fallibly human. Apparently there is an intellectual and emotional need to self-justify; a need to believe that persons of a homogenous group are superior to others. This view cannot be proven scientifically and more certainly it is not justifiable in Christian dogma.

Still, Jefferson serves as the subject of my critique and my constructive form criticism. What is more, Jefferson merely represented what many believed and still do: that people of African descent are inferior and a burden to a world solely of pale textures in the midst of a world predominately of colors.

Ironically, Jefferson wanted and possibly needed the companionship of bondsmen and women around him presumably at all times, and certainly in his crisis moments, none larger than at the time of his death. It seems that Jefferson wanted and needed his slaves closer to him than his white family but could not bring himself intellectually or emotionally to free all of them. He could not see them in every way as human as he himself was human. In an odd way, it is his duplicitous behavior that identifies him as human. "To err is human; to forgive, divine."

Jefferson's human condition is on full display when we analyze his intellectual and emotional actions toward people of African descent. This is of significant import because Jefferson's duplicity continues to be a permanent distinction of our contemporary dominating classes and cultural worldview. People of African descent are considered to be permanently relegated to permanent underclass–caste system; servants and nothing more, but to Jefferson, some of his slaves were more. Sally Hemings and her children were more; they were his emotionally and biologically more, but his psychological sense of self remained in a state of contradiction. It is his contradiction that confronts us but especially for people who believe in Eurocentric cultural hegemonic supremacist mythologies—a sense of a super-self.

Ironically, I believe that Jefferson is the quintessential human, and one of many who live with this Jeffersonian duplicity. Duplicity here is meant to be thought of alongside the Du Boisian double consciousness, which means that people are quite capable of compartmentalizing human contradictions intellectually and emotionally.[34] It has been suggested that Du Bois was informed by Henry James's sense of double consciousness:

> The use of the term "duplicity" by [Henry] James's "centre of consciousness" in this novella could be said to correspond more accurately to a *figurative* than to a *"literal* meaning of the word,"* for *duplicity* comes from the Latin *duplicitas* for "two-fold" and primarily refers to instances of doubling rather than those of deceit. The notion is on

a par with several others—such as *meaning, truth* or *reality*—the concrete and definitive interpretation of which is difficult if not impossible to pin down, particularly in the works of Henry James. If one thing is certain, however, it is that figures of "duplicity" abound in the writings of Henry James—be they fiction or non-fiction, public or private, laudatory or critical—and that duplicity is one of the key literary and rhetorical strategies within the author's vast and infamous arsenal of techniques of "ambiguity," a signature feature of the author's method more often associated with his penchant for open endings, for elusive signifiers and for systems of representation that allow for varied or even contradictory interpretations of his works.[35]

Is this at the taproot of Jeffersonian philosophy—that all people live with intellectual and emotional contradictions? If so, for Jefferson, this may point toward precisely what it means to be human.

Mr. Jefferson's University

This philosophical view of humanity may be why Jefferson wanted to advance what he envisioned to be a proper education, an education model that he felt had to be grounded in republicanism—the commitment to small and locally controlled government. His model, however, was restricted to white citizens. Jefferson's philosophy of education may mean that he concedes that all white citizens of Virginia share a common humanity and that all white humans need an education in order to grapple with their double consciousness—their duplicitous intellectual and emotional contradistinctions.

"Mr. Jefferson," as he often is called, founded the University of Virginia in 1817. His university has rightly earned its perennial academic rank among the finest institutions of higher education in the United States.[36] John Thomas Casteen III, the sixth president of the University of Virginia, writes of Jefferson, "Even more clearly than his brilliant contemporaries, Thomas Jefferson saw the necessity to educate [white] citizens and he conceived that mission broadly."[37] It is Jefferson's vision of the power of higher education which Casteen emphasizes correctly.

The University of Virginia appears to be an extension of Jefferson's mind and indirectly his double consciousness. That is, philosophically his university seeks to educate the masses, although Jefferson's philosophy of education, politics and religion is informed by his understanding of republicanism. Kevin R. C. Gutzman explains:

> Republicanism meant government by the common people, and the common people needed to be educated if they were going to govern well. "Preach," [Jefferson] told one of his close political allies, his own law teacher George Wythe, "a crusade against ignorance; establish and & improve the law for educating the common people." So Jefferson intended to do.[38]

Reason, the Benefit of the Enlightenment

Jefferson's republican ideology epitomized his sense of benefit that he believed came through the age of enlightenment. Reason was the benefit of the Enlightenment, and Jefferson wanted reason to be the cornerstone of the University of Virginia's guiding philosophy. Jefferson believed that small government was epitomized through local civic involvement, a process that enhances the knowledge of the masses to self-govern. The underclasses therefore need to be educated to assure a healthy democracy and democratic institutions. These are the rudiments of his understanding of the Enlightenment which he believed would eventually lead to a continuous evolution and maturation of the citizens of Virginia. Jefferson "could die in the comforting knowledge that there would many young men [and now women] like him—many Jeffersons [Jeffersonians]—in future generations who would probe the frontiers of knowledge, spread enlightenment, and promote moral development."[39]

Once, Jefferson made a bold statement that he supported strongly academic freedom: "This institution will be based on the illimitable freedom of the human mind. For here we are not afraid to follow truth wherever it may lead, nor tolerate any error so long as reason is left to combat it."[40] This was not true of him, however, but it was political rhetoric. Jefferson's double consciousness emerges during the hiring of the first faculty members. The original faculty came under "criticism of the European—not to mention [the] English—character of the faculty."[41] Of the original eight faculty members, only Francis Walker Gilmer was American-born, but he died before he began his tenure. After Gilmer's untimely death, "Jefferson and Madison had been particularly careful about this position [a teacher of law], because they wanted someone fully competent who also firmly shared their politics."[42] Clearly Jefferson was determined to reinforce his political and philosophical view thereon his university.[43]

Jefferson's idea of academic freedom was limited and conditioned, as well, to agree with his republican-enlightenment agenda. In short, Jefferson sought to build a university in his own human image and likeness:

> The university would have no professor of theology, for his presumptively bigoted teachings might corrupt the pure spring of republican enlightenment that he wanted his university to be. Jefferson was determined that the new law professor be an orthodox republican, if not a Republican, and that students read the right, canonical texts. One of his strongest arguments for creating the university was that it would keep Virginia boys at home: too many were matriculating at Princeton and other northern schools where they were at risk of imbibing northern (read "anti-republican") values.[44]

The current campus remains iconic and attractive but not dissimilar from other campuses that duplicated Georgian and Greek emphases that were prominent in Jefferson's time. The contemporary architecture is mixed politely and tastefully into that which was from the beginning, thus honoring the original intent of Mr. Jefferson.

Mr. Jefferson's university is a visible sign and an enduring tribute to his vision for academic excellence and accessibility for citizens seeking the finest—higher education, but his philosophy of education began much earlier. In 1787, while in Europe, Jefferson was inspired to think about the welfare of the masses, "surrounded by the passive many (the ignorant masses) and the oppressive few (the nobility and the monarchs). Division of America into two such classes must be avoided, and honing the people's intelligence was the path to avoiding it."[45]

We tend to think of the founding fathers—leaders of the revolution and early republic—as state builders first, but Jefferson had other priorities. As he put it to his closest friend and collaborator James Madison,

> Say, finally, whether peace is best preserved by giving energy to the government, or information to the people. This last is the most certain,

and the most legitimate engine of government. Educate and inform the whole mass of the people. Enable them to see that it is their interest to preserve peace and order, and they will preserve them. And it requires no very high degree of education to convince them of this. They are the only sure reliance for the preservation of our liberty.[46]

Jefferson's education is informed by classic republicanism. In short, republicanism is a government formed for and governed by common folk. For Jefferson, however, common folks need an education to understand the depth of critical and complex issues that face us every day. Of course, Jeffersonian philosophy informs what is often referred to as states' rights. This notion of local autonomy works when the citizenry is educated and therefore informed. We know that an undereducated and uneducated citizenry produces the George Wallaces and now the Donald Trumps. In our time, the powerful, who control the financial markets and other institutional spheres, manipulate the uninformed masses. In addition, Jefferson's vision works when the citizenry is homogenous. Jefferson's world is pale in textures; it is not a world where two-thirds of the world's citizens are people of color and African descent.

Slavery and the University

What remains controversial is the fact that Mr. Jefferson's university was built at the very least by free slave labor.

On July 18, 1817, construction of the University of Virginia, then called Central College, began when Jefferson assigned ten slaves to clear what had once been James Monroe's cornfield. On October 7, a day after the university's cornerstone was laid, the board of visitors met and authorized the hiring of laborers, which presumably included slaves, whites, and free blacks. Over the next nine years, these men cleared and leveled land; hauled, cut, and nailed timber; molded and fired bricks; transported quarried stone; and participated in nearly all other activities related to building the university.[47] They terraced the naturally sloping topography where the Rotunda would sit, forming an architectural apex of the Lawn. Many of the slaves were brick masons. "From the ground to the pavilions to the top of the Rotunda, slaves owned and rented by the university helped build Mr. Jefferson's Academic Village."[48]

Lucia Stanton, author of *"Those Who Labor for My Happiness"*: *Slavery at Thomas Jefferson's Monticello*, makes mention of Jefferson's use of a telescope and that it was not only for looking at celestial bodies. Instead, it was used as a way to manage his slaves' labor at Monticello and presumably during the construction of the University of Virginia. "In the 1880s, a black man who had been a Monticello slave but who had worked on the construction of the University of Virginia recalled Jefferson standing in the Monticello yard watching 'we alls at work through his spyglass.'"[49]

During the 1820s, slaves performed duties for the university's faculty and students that may be associated with dormitories but beyond; the bondsmen did all tasks associated with the students' living in well-kept quarters. Some of those duties were "fetching" water, carrying ice, stacking wood, and cleaning towels, floors, rooms, and candlesticks. They made beds, whitewashed fireplaces, and blacked students' shoes. Students did not respect slaves, often treating them rudely, often verbally and physically abusing them.[50] Many of these students came from homes that owned slaves, and many of these students wanted to bring their slaves onto campus but were not permitted to do so.[51]

Faculty members, however, could bring their slaves onto Mr. Jefferson's university campus, and often they did so. "With these professors and administrators came their slaves. The majority of the slaves living on the grounds of the university belonged to members of the faculty, almost all of whom owned or rented slaves during their time at the university."[52] Of the original professors, Bonnycastle, Dunglison (the attending physician at the time of Jefferson's death), Emmet, Harrison, Patterson, and Tucker were against slavery in principle. They attended a "fair sponsored by the ladies of the university to raise money for the Colonization Society in 1830 . . . Among themselves and in their own minds, faculty members, like Jefferson, struggled with the differences between Jeffersonian ideals and southern ideals."[53] Jefferson's double consciousness evolved into Jeffersonian double consciousness. As a result, intellectual and emotional contradictions continued at the University of Virginia.

Even though seven of the first nine professors hailed from Europe, they owned slaves. Some professors came with ideals of equality and abolitionism, but upon spending time in Charlottesville, they bent to the convenience of slave labor. Professor George Long of England purchased a slave named Jacob soon after his arrival in Charlottesville. Professor John Page Emmet, born in Ireland and raised in New York, condemned the institution of slavery, but soon after arriving at the university, he wrote John Harwell Cocke requesting assistance in purchasing a slave because he had "experienced nothing but disappointment from the hired ones. Emmet grew used to the idea of slavery, owning nine slaves, including six children, by the time of his death. Living in the university community, among professors and students steeped in the tradition of slavery, Emmet became convinced that one could hold Jeffersonian ideals and own slaves."[54]

So, how and where do we find a word of reconciliation? If we take the historical Jefferson literally and seriously, we cannot. Yet we must in this way create a bridge between Jeffersonian double consciousness and Jeffersonian and southern ideals which lifts the veil over his intellectual and emotional contradictions. Indeed Jefferson represents the quintessential human, a human riddled with double consciousness and human contradictions. The answers lie in understanding Jefferson's religious convictions that prevented him from seeing and affirming the word and ministry of reconciliation.

In the following and final chapter, I make an attempt to involve Mr. Jefferson's university in reconciling Mr. Jefferson's fallible humanity. It is his university that may bring to pass the ancient declaration that we be reconciled to God. It may do so by reinterpreting and repositioning Jefferson and Jeffersonian ideals into our globalized world and context, by implementing the twenty-first-century's ethical imperative, which is achieving human equality through closing the income and wealth gap between people of Eurocentric and African descent and other people of color.

When I left the university cemetery, I found myself overwhelmed. I needed to return to Washington, DC, before the traffic on Route 66 came to a virtual crawl. Still, I could not compartmentalize those unmarked graves that belonged to the sixty-seven. How long had their remains been there? Were they a part of the crews that cleared Monroe's cornfield? Were they among those who baked bricks of the red clay of Albemarle County that eventually became Mr. Jefferson's Rotunda?

Were they the slaves of Mr. Jefferson's initial and ensuing academic faculties, administrators, or even students? For now there is no way for us to know. But we must know, for their families' sake, for the redemption of the university and our world. Jefferson said that we must pursue truth!

Instead of traveling straight toward Washington, I found myself on Earlysville Road. Why? Because located there are the remains of some of my Virginia ancestors. Most of them were born into slavery on a local plantation. Some, after emancipation, fled the territory and came to what is now Summers County in West Virginia—some to Harper's Ferry, where they graduated from Storer College as early as 1870. Some remained in Virginia and made their homes near the plantation that once enslaved them.

What is different about these than the unfortunate sixty-seven? The difference is that my ancestors have their own cemetery and headstones and markers. Some of them were born as early as 1850. A great-great-grandmother and great-grandmother were born before those dates. They too lived on that Virginia plantation in unforgivable bondage. But what of the sixty-seven? For their sake, we must find healing and reconciliation for Charlottesville and surrounding communities, or none are healed. We look to the University of Virginia to reconcile Mr. Jefferson's double consciousness.

NOTES

1. Susan Tyler Hitchcock, *The University of Virginia: A Pictorial History* (Charlottesville: University of Virginia Press, 1999), 1.

2. Brendan Wolfe, "Unearthing Slavery at the University of Virginia: Recent Discoveries Raise New Questions about the Past," *Virginia Magazine* (spring 2013); see http://uvamagazine.org/articles/unearthing_slavery_at_the_university_of_virginia, accessed February 5, 2018.

3. Ibid., 3. Ben Ford and Steve Thomas are the principals of Rivanna Archeological Services. Ford is quoted here.

4. See https://www.monticello.org/site/research-and-collections/jefferson.

5. "Jefferson's Last Words," The Jefferson Monticello, https://www.monticello.org/site/research-and-collections/jeffersons-last-words, accessed May 26, 2017.

6. John Adams, Jefferson's moral and ideological nemesis, died later that day, July 4, 1826.

7. Ibid.

8. Ford was quoted in "Unearthing Slavery at the University of Virginia," 3.

9. C. C. Wertenbaker, *Alumni Bulletin* 4, no. 4 (1897–1898), 112. The general heading was "The University Cemetery."

10. Ibid.

11. Annette Gordon-Reed, *The Hemingses of Monticello: An American Family* (New York: Norton, 2008), 650–54.

12. John B. Boles, *Jefferson: Architect of American Liberty* (New York: Basic Books, 2017), 513–16.

13. Annette Gordon-Reed and Peter S. Onuf, *"Most Blessed of the Patriarchs": Thomas Jefferson and the Empire of the Imagination* (New York: Liveright, 2016), 301.

14. Ibid., 315.

15. Amalgamation is similar to miscegenation, the subject of *Loving v. Virginia* (1967). See Cornell University Law School, https://www.law.cornell.edu/supremecourt/text/388/1, accessed May 17, 2017.

16. "Inaugural Address of Governor George Wallace, Which Was Delivered at the Capitol in Montgomery, Alabama," Alabama Department of Archives and History, http://digital.archives.alabama.gov/cdm/ref/collection/voices/id/2952, accessed May 26, 2017. The speech was delivered in 1963.

17. W. E. B. Du Bois, *The Souls of Black Folk* (New York: Bantam, 2005), 3.

18. John Ferling, *Jefferson and Hamilton: The Rivalry That Forged a Nation* (New York: Bloomsbury Press, 2013), 165.

19. Du Bois, *Souls of Black Folk*, 3.

20. Gordon-Reed and Onuf, *"Most Blessed of the Patriarchs,"* 5.

21. Henry Wiencek, *Master of the Mountain: Thomas Jefferson and His Slaves* (New York: Farrar, Straus and Giroux, 2012), 44–45.

22. Ibid.

23. Ibid., 45.

24. I have witnessed a Jefferson-like double consciousness among white southerners and Appalachians. It is this double consciousness that causes poor and sociomarginalized whites from America's south and Appalachia to suffer from sociopsychological schisms and manipulations, recently witnessed in the outcome of the 2016 United States presidential election. It is claimed that many thought "Obama Care" and the Affordable Care Act (ACA) are different programs. To recognize that they are the same would mean the graduate of Columbia University and Harvard Law School Barack Obama, was equal to them and had helped them. In defense of Eurocentric racial mythologies, this was inconceivable. Like contemporary southerners and Appalachians, Jefferson did not confront his intellectual and emotional contradictions.

25. Jefferson "recalled that his first memory was being handed up on a pillow to be carried by a slave on horseback." Gordon-Reed, *The Hemingses of Monticello*, 94.

26. Wiencek, *Master of the Mountain*, 51.

27. Henry Louis Gates Jr., *The Signifying Monkey: A Theory of African-American Literary Criticism* (Oxford: Oxford University Press, 1988), 73.

28. Ibid., 141–42.

29. Cornel West, *The Cornel West Reader* (New York: Basic Civitas Books, 1999), 82.

30. Ellery Washington, "Seeing the Paris of James Baldwin," *Seattle Times* (February 7, 2014). See http://www.seattletimes.com/life/travel/seeing-the-paris-of-james-baldwin/, accessed May 26, 2017.

31. Thomas Jefferson, *Notes on the State of Virginia* (New York: Penguin Books, 1999), 145–47.

32. Gordon-Reed, *The Hemingses of Monticello*, 124.

33. Ibid.

34. Du Bois, *Souls of Black Folk*, 3.

35. Dennis Tredy, "A 'Curious Duplicity,'" editor's preface, in *Henry James and the Poetics of Duplicity*, ed. Dennis Tredy, Annick Duperray, and Adrian Harding (Newcastle upon Tyne, England: Cambridge Scholars Publishing, 2013), viii.

36. According to *US News & World Report*, the University of Virginia is ranked #24 (tie) among national universities in 2017. See https://www.usnews.com/best-colleges/uva-6968, accessed May 2, 2017.

37. John Thomas Casteen III, quoted in Hitchcock, *University of Virginia*. For this book, Dr. Casteen wrote his perspective of Jefferson's vision of liberal arts education.

38. Kevin R. C. Gutzman, *Thomas Jefferson, Revolutionary: A Radical's Struggle to Remake America* (New York: St. Martin's Press, 2017), 195–96.

39. Gordon-Reed and Onuf, *"Most Blessed of the Patriarchs,"* 296.

40. Boles, *Jefferson*, 497.

41. Ibid., 496.

42. Ibid.

43. Ibid. "One suspects that their [Jefferson's and James Madison's] memories of the bitter political controversies of the 1790s simply overwhelmed their commitment to complete intellectual freedom" (497).

44. Gordon-Reed and Onuf, *"Most Blessed of the Patriarchs,"* 278–79.

45. Gutzman, *Thomas Jefferson, Revolutionary*, 196.

46. Ibid.

47. See *Encyclopedia Virginia*, http://www.encyclopediavirginia.org/Slavery_at_the_University_of_Virginia#start_entry, accessed May 22, 2017.

48. Catherine S. Neale, "Slaves, Freedpeople and the University of Virginia," senior thesis paper for partial fulfillment of the requirements for the

Degree of Arts with honors (April 14, 2006), 12. https://libraetd.lib.virginia
.edu/public_view/1v53jx044, accessed March 21, 2018.

49. Lucia Stanton, *"Those Who Labor for My Happiness": Slavery at Thomas Jefferson's Monticello* (Charlottesville: University of Virginia Press, 2012), 100.

50. See *Encyclopedia Virginia*.

51. Neale, "Slaves, Freedpeople and the University of Virginia," 7.

52. Ibid., 28.

53. Ibid.

54. Ibid., 29.

Pure Religion

James 1:27, Illumination, and Reconciling Fallible Humanity

For his tombstone at Monticello, Thomas Jefferson left specific instructions on how he wanted to be remembered: as "Author of the Declaration of American Independence / of the Statute of Virginia for Religious Freedom / and Father of the University of Virginia."[1]

Thomas Jefferson was a brilliant man. Anyone who denies this fact lacks intellectual integrity and very likely moral honesty. Jefferson's contributions to the birth of his nation are undeniable, even though it remains an imperfect union. His authorship of the United States Declaration of Independence and the Virginia Statute for Religious Freedom and his fatherhood of the University of Virginia set him apart and legitimately position him among American icons (not to mention that he was the third president of the United States). Jefferson shares space with persons such as Abraham Lincoln, Alexander Crummell, W. E. B. DuBois, Mordecai Wyatt Johnson, Lyndon Baines Johnson, Martin Luther King Jr., Shirley Chisholm, and the like.

Still, Jefferson was a fallible human being. The task then is to find a way to reconcile Jeffersonian idealism with his human abuses of socio-oppressed people of African descent—namely, Jefferson's own slaves. One way to consider this is to explain to him and his Jeffersonian idealists the ministry of reconciliation. First, I must place Jefferson (and Jeffersonian) double consciousness front and center without attaching double consciousness to Mr. Jefferson. There is no credible way to grasp his sense of self and his sense of human superiority over people who were and are not of white European origin.

With this in mind, we cannot merely accept that Jefferson was a man of his age—a man who was influenced and conditioned by the Enlightenment—as a plausible explanation for his racist worldview. It is more plausible to suggest that like many others, his double consciousness enabled him to compartmentalize his intellectual and emotional contradictions. For whites, double consciousness incubates racial mythologies of superiorities and inferiorities in spite of evidences that will not support these mythologies. What is more, there is a corollary relationship that exists between Jefferson's religious worldview and his double consciousness that prevented him from acknowledging human equality among races and genders of people.

The Religious Worldview of Jefferson

For a religious worldview, I turn to the New Testament: "Religion that is pure and undefiled before God, the Father, is this: to care for orphans and widows in their distress, and to keep oneself unstained by the world" (James 1:27, NRSV). Pure religion is a worldview that points toward our human dependence on "otherness," that is, a unique divine actor who is above human fallibility. Still, the divine actor is involved intimately in our human liberation struggle. Second, this religious worldview points toward human interdependence. In other words, and quite literally, people are obligated to care for others regardless of their race, gender, and other human orientations. Biblical religion is a vertical and horizontal relationship between God with humanity and humanity with humanity. Jefferson understood and accepted that the religion of Jesus is both ethical and moral. For Jefferson, however, that was as far as the religion of Jesus was intended to go. Jefferson did not embrace traditional orthodox views that Jesus of Nazareth is incarnate divinity. Jefferson's religion did not align with that which James 1:7 proclaims is "pure religion."

An example of pure religion is such that humans are not motivated by self-interest. Instead, pure religion comes of a willingness to involve ourselves in the lives of the most vulnerable people in our societies; we search for ways to reconcile our human differences whether those differences are caused by class, race, gender, or human orientations. In the world of the apostle James, reconciliation is exemplified when we reconcile power with the powerless, such as widows and orphans. This philanthropic spirit is motivated and inspired by the presence and work of the Holy Spirit, the third person of the Godhead. The Holy Spirit inspires participation in the ministry of reconciliation. It seems this is what Jefferson lacked. His religion did not include a benevolent point of departure, namely, that Jesus of Nazareth is benevolent and more than human, that Jesus was and is the second person in the Godhead. Jefferson refused to believe in a trinitarian concept of God. Jefferson's Jesus is solely of human nature and not otherworldly. To believe in the otherworldliness of Jesus, Jefferson would have had to embrace transcendence, which is another way to say that Jefferson would have had to accept the unexplainable, the possibility of miracles. A miracle by definition is transcendence.

Jefferson's religion was shaped by his immersion in human reason and condensed to constructs of ethical and moral principles. These principles then were evangelized to support enlightened human reason. That is, human reason grounds many sects of religious idealism and practices. Jefferson's religion was commonplace among Enlightenment intellectuals on both sides of the Atlantic. Ideologically, Jefferson's elitism and religion were racist and supremacist. In my view, without Christian conversion it is nearly impossible to overcome racism and other forms of hegemonic supremacist idealisms.

By contrast, Christian conversion usurps the conclusion of human reason that there exist a superior race and inferior races of people. An example of this is evidenced in Peter's life (Acts 10:44-48). Christian conversion is revelatory. In fact, a major part of the Christian experience is our claim that Scripture is significant; that the canon of Scripture is revelation; and that Christians (that is, those converted by the Word and Spirit) come to know that Jews and Gentiles are equal parts of the whole, the human family. What is more, Christians continue to mature through the illuminating light that is the Spirit of Christ. It is the Spirit who reveals the double consciousness that functions in all people.

Later in the New Testament we read about the apostle Peter's double consciousness. Peter's life at one point is a picture of what a racial supremacist ideology is (Galatians 2:11-14). Peter, however, continues to mature, as evidenced by the writings of his pastorals. There readers are gratified to see that he became a man who understood what the apostle Paul came to know: there are no differences between people (Galatians 3:28; cf. 1 Peter 1:13-17). We do not read that Thomas Jefferson had similar experiences of Pauline and Petrine regeneration and sanctification. Instead, regrettably, we do find evidence that throughout Jefferson's public career, he seldom spoke about his personal and private religious worldview. Nevertheless, Jefferson left markers so that we may make informed characterizations of his religious ideaology.

> Jefferson considered liberty of conscience to be the basis of all other freedom. He held to this position fervently from his earliest surviving comments on the subject to the end of his days. His role in establishing Virginia's devotion to it stood for him among his most significant achievements. He ranked it with writing the Declaration of Independence and establishing the University of Virginia, including it with them on his gravestone.[2]

Of Jefferson Kevin R.C. Gutzman said, "we have no evidence to substantiate the idea that [he] was ever a Trinitarian—that is, a Christian."[3] Jefferson did claim to be a Christian, but he did not accept traditional orthodoxy: "I am a Christian, in the only sense in which he [Jesus] wished any one to be; sincerely attached to his doctrines, in preference to all others; ascribing to himself every human excellence, and believing he never claimed any other."[4] Jefferson thought that Jesus was very human but not very God, and therefore Jefferson refused to ascribe to the biblical Jesus co-equality with the Father and Holy Spirit, which is a trinitarian worldview. Jefferson's religion was grounded solely in human reason, or humanism.

So committed was he to his humanism, it informed his religious worldview. This is significant and further shapes a context for two of Jefferson's important and interrelated contributions to American liberal society. These contributions are the Virginia Statute for Religious Freedom and what later became commonly called The Jefferson Bible. The Virginia Statute for Religious Freedom can be summarized in the following way:

> In 1786 a bill finally made its way through the Virginia House of Delegates. The law guaranteed Presbyterians, Baptists, and other sects in Virginia the freedom to worship, stating, "No man [or woman] shall be

compelled to frequent or support religious worship place, or ministry whatsoever, nor shall be enforced, restrained, molested or burthened in his body of goods, nor shall otherwise suffer on account of his religious opinions or belief." With this provision, the law moved beyond protecting rights of dissenters to include those of deists, skeptics, and those with no religion at all. It certainly showed the stamp of Jefferson authorship.[5]

Historian John B. Boles characterizes Jefferson's statute of religious freedom as an act of tolerance. "His notes [Jefferson's] contain such paraphrases of [John] Locke as 'no man has power to let another prescribe his faith' and '[church] is a voluntary society of men.'"[6] In this context, Jefferson reacted against support of a state church, something that is commonly known as religious establishment. "Over the course of the next several years, dissenters—again, especially Baptists—sent scores of petitions to the [Virginia] legislature protesting their oppression and calling for religious freedom and disestablishment of the Anglican Church," which was state-supported by a compulsory tax.[7] This protest seemed reasonable to Jefferson. His statute then was aligned with his Enlightenment ideals—the freedom of conscience.

The freedom of conscience was the Enlightenment mantra which Jefferson defended wholeheartedly. As we will see later, freedom of conscience was Jefferson's philosophical and foundational influence that shaped his vision of a utilitarian University of Virginia. But was there more to Jefferson's freedom of conscience motives? Jefferson's religious worldview did not include intellectual space for transcendence. This was seen clearly in Jefferson's utter rejection of the biblical Evangelists' claims that Jesus performed miracles. For Jefferson, miracles were added to embellish the ethical and moral teachings of Jesus—and what is more, according to Jefferson, accepting miracles as a part of his reality would be an unintended acknowledgment that he believed superstitions.[8]

The Jefferson Bible and the Influence of David Hume

The second seminal contribution that Jefferson made to American liberal society was his controversial *Life and Morals of Jesus of Nazareth Extracted Textually from the Gospels in Greek, Latin, French, and English*, which was completed in 1820. Jefferson's commitment to human reason apparently would not permit him to accept consciously the biblical Evangelists' claims about the divinity of Jesus and their suprarational claims of him. Jefferson's Gospel extracts seem to have been influenced by the teachings of David Hume. Hume was Scottish born and educated at the University of Edinburgh. Ernest C. Mossner described Hume this way:

> David Hume is the greatest of British philosophers, and his greatness, it is now believed, reveals itself most strikingly in the first as well as the most sustained and systematic of his works: *A Treatise of Human Nature*. Berkeley published his *New Theory of Vision* (1709) when he was twenty-four and *A Treatise of the Principles of Human Knowledge* a year later . . . the appearance of the three volumes of Hume's *Treatise* by the time he was twenty-nine still warrants a claim for the author's outstanding philosophical precocity. . . . Modern readers, however, are likely to be deeply moved and teased into thought by the elements in the *Treatise* which haunted the mature Hume: the nakedness of intellectual self-exposure, the provocative assaults on established systems, and the aggressive presentation of a revolutionary account of man's nature. With justice Sir Isaiah Berlin has written of Hume: "No man has influenced the history of philosophy to a deeper and more disturbing degree."[9]

Cornel West has a harsh criticism of Hume's philosophical writings: "Hume's racism was notorious; it served as a major source of proslavery arguments and antiblack education propaganda."[10] West cites the following excerpt from Hume's essay "Of National Characters" as an example:

> I am apt to suspect the negroes, and in general all other species of men (for there are four or five different kinds) to be naturally inferior to the whites. There never was a civilized nation of any other complexion than white, nor even any individual eminent either in action or speculation. No ingenious manufactures amongst them, no arts, no sciences. . . .
>   In Jamaica indeed they talk of one negroe [*sic*] as a man of learning; but 'tis likely he is admired for very slender accomplishments, like a parrot, who speaks a few words plainly.[11]

Henry Louis Gates Jr. notes that Hume's racism may have reinforced that of Jefferson. What is certain, the racist views of Hume and Jefferson parallel. "The eighteenth century abounds in comments from philosophers such as David Hume in 'Of National Characters' and statesmen such as Thomas Jefferson in *Notes on the State of Virginia*, who argued that blacks were 'imitative' rather than 'creative.'"[12]

Hume's influence upon Jefferson is palpable. On the one hand, Hume writes, "In Jamaica indeed they talk of one Negroe [*sic*] as a man of learning; but 'tis likely he is admired for very slender accomplishments, like a parrot, who speaks a few words plainly," and on the other Jefferson writes in *Notes*:

> But never yet could I find that a black had uttered a thought above the level of plain narration: never see even an elementary trait of painting or sculpture. In music they are more generally gifted than the whites with accurate ears for tune and time, and they have been found capable of imagining a small catch. Whether they will be equal to the composition of a more extensive run of melody, or of complicated harmony, is yet to be proved. Misery is often the parent of the most effecting touches in poetry. —Among the blacks is misery enough, God knows, but no poetry. Love is a peculiar oestrum of the poet. Their love is ardent, but it kindles the senses only, not the imagination. Religion indeed has produced a Phyllis [Phillis] Whately [Wheatley]; but it could not produce a poet. The compositions published under her name are below dignity of criticism.[13]

In these instances, West and Gates point toward racial hegemonic supremacist views that are located in Hume's and Jefferson's literary work. Gates, however, correctly points to that which I have determined to be the loci for Jefferson's *Notes*. I have also determined that Hume's religious worldview influenced that of Jefferson. Hume, like "participants in the Enlightenment[,] applied the critical force of human reason to test received knowledge about the natural, social, and moral worlds," and "Jefferson and many of his correspondents embraced the exhilarating prospect of liberating their contemporaries' minds from inherited misconceptions and superstitions."[14]

In 1748, Hume wrote what is considered "the most celebrated article written to refute the possibility of transcendence" into the "natural, social and moral worlds." Hume dismissed the possibility of biblical miracles as nothing more than superstitions. In his essay, Hume sets forth an argument against belief in miracles that "provoked a lively response in his day, and it has continued to be the subject of vigorous dispute up to the present day."[15]

> Nothing is so convenient as a decisive argument of this kind, which must at least silence the most arrogant bigotry and superstition, and free us from their impertinent solicitations. I flatter myself, that I have discovered an argument of like nature, which, if just, will, with the wise and learned, be an everlasting check to all kinds of superstitious delusion, and consequently, will be useful as long as the world endures. For so long, I presume, will the accounts of miracles and prodigies be found in all history, sacred and profane.[16]

Hume confirms and defends what he believes, which is that the universe is a closed system. Hume's philosophical and religious worldview does not include intellectual space for transcendence. His enslavement to human reason does not permit him to find other means to interpret historical human and biblical events through otherworldly pheromones. In short, miracles cannot be affirmed as rational possibilities because miracles are offensive to those bound to human reason. Therefore, by human reason alone, Hume rejects the possibilities of the literal existence of miracles. Jefferson did the same. From his Bible, Jefferson extracted the passages that mention miracles which the Evangelists included.

As early as 1804, fifty-six years after Hume's "Against Miracles" was published, and eighteen years after the Virginia Statute for Religious Freedom was passed by the Virginia House of Delegates, Jefferson began to think philosophically about what would become known later as the Jefferson Bible. Jefferson would "rid the gospel message of those aspects that appeared to him as 'contrary to reason,' leaving behind only the 'authentic' story of Jesus."[17]

Jefferson shared his religious views sparingly. He did have correspondence with Joseph Priestly, an English theologian and scientist. "Jefferson joined with Priestly and others in seeking to establish humanity's moral duties and determine the role of religion in promoting them."[18] Priestly, whose *An History of the Corruptions of Christianity* was published in 1782, considered doctrines of the Trinity, original sin, and predestination as corruptions of the Bible and therefore manipulations of the human reason of Christians and citizens of societies at large. "He believed that such teachings prevented people from understanding and embracing Christian faith and that authorities multiplied the mysteries of religion and promulgated superstitions."[19]

Jefferson shared his religious views with the respected Dr. Benjamin Rush, a Philadelphia physician, scientist, humanitarian, member of the Continental Congress, and disciple of the Enlightenment. Rush was a devout Christian and a member of the Presbyterian denomination. He did not agree with Jefferson's religious views: "The discussion [between Jefferson and Rush] must sometimes have been contentious, for it uncovered stark differences of opinion."[20]

Jefferson also was associated with Thomas Paine, the author of *The Age of Reason*, "which powerfully argued Paine's deist beliefs in God as a maker, while rejecting the divinity of Jesus and denouncing clerical power."[21] This association did not occur without public notice and disapproval. In 1802, Paine was President Thomas Jefferson's guest in Washington. "Critics associated Jefferson with Paine's most unpopular views on Christianity as a way to lessen the Republican president's pubic support."[22]

Influenced by his conversations with Priestley, Rush, and Paine (and I must not overlook the obvious, which is Hume), Jefferson created what he called a syllabus that later would evolve into the Jefferson Bible:

> The "Syllabus" thus described humankind's moral progress. At the same time, it also expressed Jefferson's view that the New Testament itself provided only an imperfect transmission of the finest of Jesus's teachings. Jesus had not written his teachings himself, and his disciples, Jefferson believed, had been largely illiterate and unsophisticated men. In addition, Jesus had faced the crushing opposition of the learned and powerful of his day, who suppressed his message as they cut short his life. Well after Jesus's lifetime, powerful interests found their own advantage "in sophisticating and perverting the simple doctrines he taught." Like Priestley's work, then, the "Syllabus" laid emphasis on the corruptions of Jesus's contributions to human ethics.[23]

Jefferson's syllabus became the outline that eventually would guide his extraction of the miracles and assertions that Jesus is co-equal with the Trinitarian God. This text is a primary source and window into the religious mind of Thomas Jefferson. "By removing all references to superstition and the supernatural, Jefferson made clear his admiration of Jesus as a great teacher and moral philosopher while, at the same time, reaffirming his belief in the commitment to the power of reason as the basis for understanding life and the natural world."[24] In his version of the Gospels, Jefferson was audacious and bold if not arrogant and borderline heretical. He cut parts of the Gospel narratives:

> Left behind in the source material were those elements that he could not support through reason, that he believed were later embellishments, or what seemed superfluous or repetitious across the Four Evangelists' accounts. Absent are the annunciation, the resurrection, the water turned to wine, and the multitudes fed on five loaves of bread and two fishes. It essentially offers what the title indicates: a distillation of the teachings of Jesus the moral reformer, combined with what Jefferson accepted as the historical facts pertaining to Jesus the man.[25]

This is a portrait of Jefferson's philosophical and religious worldviews. Jefferson was grounded in the age of reason—the Enlightenment, which is humanism. Nevertheless, he gave Americans religious freedom and he gave Americans freedom from religion. This freedom protects the orthodoxy of Christians who embrace miracles and the divinity of Jesus. It protects persons of all religious sects; it protects the agnostic and the atheist from the power of an established state religion in the United States. What I want to embellish is that Jefferson was protecting himself. That is, Jefferson assured himself legal protection from the state. Jefferson's religious views placed him in the minority among Virginians. If Jefferson's religious views had been vetted and critiqued beyond suspicions thereof, his political career may have ended prematurely. It is believed widely that Jefferson had been considered less than a competent governor of Virginia.[26]

Nonetheless, his personal commitments to human reason place Jefferson's religiosity and his Jeffersonian idealism under the light of the world's scrutiny. Jefferson was the consummate master of political strategy, tactics, and calculus. His views were out of step with majorities of Virginians and eventually American voters. Jefferson therefore kept his religious views private; today, Jefferson would be considered an agnostic. What is important and critical to my argument is that Jefferson's double consciousness emerges in his intellectual and emotional contradictions.

The Implications of Jefferson's Religious Views

At outset of this chapter, I asserted that our task was to find a way to reconcile Mr. Jefferson and his Jeffersonian idealism against those he had wronged, namely, people of African descent and specifically his slaves. To them I now add the sixty-seven slaves who were introduced in chapter 6, whose remains were discovered in unmarked graves in the University of Virginia cemetery in 2012. For the most part, they are nameless, faceless, and without ethical, moral, and legal recourse. They cannot speak for themselves.

Jefferson's Declaration of Independence, the Virginia Statute for Religions Freedom, and the founding of the University of Virginia are interconnecting and define Jeffersonian idealism. Jeffersonian idealism was not meant to address the welfare of people of African descent because Mr. Jefferson and Jeffersonian idealism do not see human equality in black humanity.

This adds immediacy to our task to reconcile Mr. Jefferson and his Jeffersonian idealism because of its globalized sociopolitical and religious implications. Moreover, how is Jeffersonian idealism meant to be understood in our contemporary culture? Nations have made attempts to emulate Jeffersonian idealism—and directly and indirectly emulated Jefferson's double consciousness and his intellectual and emotional contradictions. Thus Jeffersonian idealism continues to promote indifference toward people of African descent in a global context.

Jefferson's racist indifference coupled with his political and religious worldviews did not then or now protect the rights and privileges of people of African descent in America and ultimately in the world. Jefferson's double consciousness, to which I believe contemporary Jeffersonian idealism can be traced, distorted his worldview and prevented him from seeing and accepting the equality of sociomarginalized people with people who were born into the white race. We see a second demarcation when Eurocentric-dominating classes and culture are considered. I conclude therefore that neither Jefferson nor his ideals can be reconciled by the man himself. So, how do we reconcile Jefferson and Jeffersonian idealism in the face of past and present human abuses?

I believe this can be accomplished by appealing to his university. The University of Virginia appears to be an extension of Mr. Jefferson's republican idealism and his humanism. An appeal to his university is an effort to reconcile Mr. Jefferson's double consciousness that surfaces through his intellectual and emotional contradictions. Later we shall look to Mr. Jefferson's university as his catalyst for the ministry of reconciliation in the twenty-first-century global context.

At the time of this writing, Teresa A. Sullivan is president of the University of Virginia. Sullivan wrote in the foreword to the second edition of *The University of Virginia: A Pictorial History*:

> Thomas Jefferson's plan for the University of Virginia was as bold and revolutionary as his plan for the American republic he helped to conceive. The nation's founding and this university's founding are intertwining stories in our national narrative. The new nation promised liberty to its citizens, and this university provided education to ensure the preservation of that liberty. Mr. Jefferson wrote, "If a nation expects to be ignorant and free, in a state of civilization, it expects what never was and never will be." He designed his university to foster practical learning that would banish ignorance, ensuring freedom for all.[27]

Of course Jefferson's plan for his university did not include people of African descent and other sociomarginalized people. His plan did not include women as students, faculty, or staff. He did not envision that Sullivan would be the university's first (white) female president. But Mr. Jefferson's university did own and rent slaves to build its edifices. Faculty members and students owned slaves, and the faculty's slaves lived on the campus to meet their oppressors' needs.

Recently, the University of Virginia rightly renamed one of its student dormitories after two university slaves. This was in response to the unearthing of the sixty-seven slaves' graves in 2012. Subtle changes have been made in the university culture, as noted in the *News and Advance* newspaper article entitled "UVa Names Dorm after Former Slaves": "The university officially christened Gibbons House, a dorm on the Alderman Road that will house about 200 first year students . . . Naming the dorm in honor of William and Isabella Gibbons—who were owned by UVa professors—is a part of an effort by the administration to acknowledge the history of slavery on the UVa Grounds."[28]

This article describes William Gibbons and Isabella Gibbons as literate, each learning to read though it was illegal at the time for slaves to be taught to read. Isabella became a teacher (she taught at the Freedmen's School, now known as the Jefferson School), and William became a pastor of two notable churches (the First Baptist Church of Charlottesville and the Zion Baptist Church in Washington, DC). These are thoughtful and appropriate changes in the university's culture. However, these changes did not result in economic reparations. The surviving descendants of William and Isabella have not received restorative restitution at the time of this writing.

It is imperative to reintroduce our thesis: *Effective twenty-first-century preaching is prophetic when it addresses closing the income and wealth gap.*[29] Because of antebellum slavery and today, racialized immigration reform and an obviously immoral disproportionate incarceration rate of people of African descent, the economic impact on the black community is nearing genocidal levels. The University of Virginia must do more to reconcile Mr. Jefferson and his Jeffersonian idealism, which reinforces his double consciousness and intellectual and emotional contradictions.

According to *College Factual*, the University of Virginia's racial diversity is as follows: whites are 61.3 percent of students; interestingly, the pie chart does not provide further percentages. It appears Asian students are the largest percentage of non-white students. African American, Hispanic/Latino, Non-resident Alien, and Ethnic Identity Unknown student percentages appear to be nearly if not equally the same.[30] *College Atlas* lists similar percentages: white are 60 percent, Asians are 12 percent, black or African American are 7 percent, Hispanic/Latino are 5 percent, Race/Ethnicity unknown are 7 percent and Non-resident Alien are 6 percent of the student body.[31]

White student enrollment at Mr. Jefferson's university is six out of ten. Black student enrollment at Mr. Jefferson's university is less than one out of ten. This is unacceptable. The slave history at the University of Virginia and the Commonwealth's segregation laws alone make this untenable. A ghostly white fact is that Mr. Jefferson's and other planters' slaves built the university's buildings and infrastructure without wages and economic compensation. This is unethical and immoral. Furthermore, this indicates that contemporary advocates of Jeffersonian idealism have inherited Jefferson's double consciousness. These statistical data point toward Jeffersonian intellectual and emotional contradictions.

Ben Myers, in "The Flagship Diversity Divide," writes, "The student bodies at large state universities are more diverse than the faculties. But the broader population outpaces them both."[32] Myers provided a chart that used careful measurement indicators. "At most flagships, there is a significant disparity between the diversity of the student body and the diversity of the faculty. In fact, institutions with the greatest student diversity have the largest such gaps. Only eight institutions, or 16 percent, have faculty more diverse than the student body."[33]

Racial diversity is often debated. What is undebatable is that Mr. Jefferson's university must work harder than most schools because of its white supremacist past. The university rhetoric does not reflect its admissions and enrollment realities. Myers and the *Chronicle of Higher Education* developed a Diversity Index. The index "represents the probability that any two people chosen at random from a sample will be of different races or ethnicities. The index works on a scale of zero to 100. A score of zero means that there's no chance that those two people will be of different races; a score of 100 means it's guaranteed that they will be."[34]

My interest here is delimited to the University of Virginia and its student-professor ratio. More clearly, I mean the ratio between the racial and ethnic diversity of the University of Virginia's full-time professors compared with the racial and ethnic diversity of the University of Virginia's full-time students. *The Chronicle*'s bar graph shows that for every 58.5 ethnically and racially diverse students attending the University of Virginia, there are only 25.5 ethnically and racially diverse full-time professors serving on the University of Virginia faculty. The gap is one of the largest of the flagship schools included in the study.

In fact, the graph indicates that the University of Virginia is in a three-way tie for the fourth-worst flagship state school for its lack of a diverse faculty-to-student ratio (-22%) Those that are behind Mr. Jefferson's university are the University of Nevada, the University of California Berkeley, and the University of Georgia. The Commonwealth of Virginia's diversity is 53 percent, and the University of Virginia's faculty's diversity is 31 percent. Student diversity at Mr. Jefferson's university is 55 percent. The University of Virginia's faculty is 22 percent below the Commonwealth's population diversity. These statistics suggest that the University of Virginia's rhetoric does not match its actions. What is more, these statistics signify the continuation of Mr. Jefferson's double consciousness and intellectual and emotional contradictions.

To its credit, the University of Virginia published a report called the President's Commission on Slavery and the University, which I assume was inspired and commissioned in response to the unearthing of the sixty-seven slave graves.[33] The report begins with citing the actions of other prominent universities: Brown University's Committee on Slavery and Justice (2006); Emory University's Conference on Examining the History and Legacy of Slavery's Role in Higher Education (2011, one year before the University of Virginia's inadvertent discovery of sixty-seven slave graves on its campus); and the University of North Carolina's Slavery and the Making of the University (on exhibit in 2005–2006).[36]

In addition to the president's commission, the University of Virginia is a catalyst for Universities Studying Slavery, a consortium of schools committed to exploring the ramifications on the institutions. At this time, none of these universities have made financial restitutions to descendants of the slaves who either built these universities' infrastructures or served as slaves on their campuses without financial compensation. University cultures must be held accountable; their studies are another way to describe a process—something for the majorities. In this instance, the majorities were not injured. The minorities were injured and without recourse. In short, university studies are a democratic process; the conclusive reports are not legal and binding; their reports do not bring remedy to the injured; their reports do not find its writers guilty of crimes and misdemeanors. It is a process that is insulting to people of African descent. Where is the justice? What is the justice?

Reconciling Jefferson's Humanity

Apparently the University of Virginia did not take its initial actions to begin its democratic process until after the dreadful discovery. Certainly Mr. Jefferson's university was the last to do so among those universities that are listed as a part of the University of Virginia commission's opening statement. Neither citing the actions of other universities nor characterizing them as equally culpable accomplishes positive actions and results. Neither does the commission report become Mr. Jefferson's university. The onus remains with the University of Virginia because it is Mr. Jefferson's university.

The University of Virginia should not meet the standard but exceed it, precisely because it is the university that Mr. Jefferson founded. Naming dormitories after deceased slaves does not benefit their living descendants or other people of African descent whose deceased forebears were enslaved for their entire lives. Is this justice in a capitalistic society? Is this fair in any way when it is clear that generations of dominating classes of the dominating culture continue to benefit through the sweat and toil of unrewarded people, a people who have nothing to show for their labor? What is of vital importance is that we understand that slaves have nothing to pass along to their descendants except the stigmatized burden of being sons and daughters of slaves. Mr. Jefferson died in 1826 with double consciousness and intellectual and emotional contradictions. In 2018, it appears that his university continues to adhere to his Jeffersonian idealism and too continues to be enslaved with his double consciousness and intellectual and emotional contradictions.

Only the University of Virginia can reconcile Mr. Jefferson's humanity. It will take an imaginary revision of the last days that Mr. Jefferson lived surrounded by his two families. Mr. Jefferson must be remade as a fallible man who understood and accepted the biblical mandate, the ministry of reconciliation. This imaginary revision provides reconciling space for Mr. Jefferson's university to change the course of the future, but it must be bold and intentional in its reconciling actions. What does the university gain? It addresses Jeffersonian double consciousness and its intellectual and emotional contradictions that continue to cause suspicion from people of African descent and other people of color around the globe. The University of Virginia can reconcile Mr. Jefferson with his slaves' descendants through tangible economic reparations in a restorative manner. How does this imaginary revision of Mr. Jefferson take place?

What if Thomas Jefferson were not a deist? What if Jefferson would have accepted the miraculous power of the gospel and could withstand no longer his own spiritual conversion and transformation? Then Jefferson would have embraced the Old and New Testaments as justice motifs, narratives of liberation and reconciliation (in that order). The story of reconciliation would be different. Jefferson might have prevented centuries of strife and struggle. As a spiritually converted follower of Jesus of Nazareth, Jefferson would have had a different discussion with his slaves during his last earthly moments. The nation may have avoided the Civil War and the civil rights struggles that ensued and caused countless people to lose their lives in quest of their freedom, liberty, and equality.

Let us suppose that at the very least, Burwell Colbert, Joseph Fossett, Elizabeth, Sally, and Madison Hemings, and Wormley Hughes were around Jefferson's deathbed. Let us imagine that Jefferson indeed spoke a word of reconciliation to them, that he admitted to them that he had come to terms with his double consciousness and his intellectual and emotional contradictions. That he further explained that over the years and more recently, "I have read tenderly the apostle Paul's second Corinthian epistle, and I can no longer escape its exegetical quality, its expositional beauty and truth that it has borne. I concede to the very reasons for which Paul has written."

Let us imagine that when his eyes and heart fell upon 2 Corinthians 5:16-20, Jefferson understood what Paul had explained. Because Jefferson was literate in biblical Greek, he trembled as the illuminating light of the Holy Spirit caught him and lifted the veil from his eyes and heart. For the first time, he understood that reconciliation is an evolving process. What if Jefferson had admitted to his slaves that the word of reconciliation is a ministry? That Jefferson admitted the ministry of reconciliation is a fiduciary and ethical duty to be "reconciled to God" (2 Corinthians 5:11-20)? From the light of that Pauline passage, Jefferson accepts that he has been given the grace and stewardship to reconcile with those he has wronged. Jefferson no doubt would have called his white family alongside his slaves and said, "No longer do I call you slaves" but friends and family (John 15:15, NASB). What would have been different if Jefferson would have said, "I have wronged all of you and therefore I repent"?

What if Jefferson would have uttered the words, "I must free all slaves and ask that all work together to retire all of my indebtedness"? What might have happened if Jefferson would have said to his white and black families, "You are now one family, and together you will change the world"? If only Mr. Jefferson said to Nicholas Trist, his granddaughter's husband, "I want you to make certain that all of my slaves' descendants who are qualified academically are educated at my university. I want you to commission future presidents that a part of their obligation is to create a scholarship endowment for that purpose and place a strong emphasis on science, mathematics, engineering, and technology. This will be important for the future of this country that I helped found." And, "Trist, you make sure that we have the most diverse faculty in the world—this will be a start. Someday millions of people will know that I acknowledge that I am sorry for my earthly actions that enslaved humans of my same body and quality."

Of course, we do not believe that this conversation took place (unless Thomas Jefferson Randolph chose not to repeat it). This conversation, however, is an ethical speculation of ongoing conversations that must take place continuously at the University of Virginia. The university must find the descendants of the sixty-seven slaves who are buried in unmarked graves near the university campus. The university's administration and board of visitors must seek ways to reconcile with the ashen ghosts of Jefferson's past that remain between the slaves, their unmarked graves, and their rest and justice. Reconciliation here is nothing less than human justice, which is economic reparations in some form. The university must prepare for retribution and restorative justice and get in front of the growing groundswell across the width and breadth of our nation.

Nevertheless, Jefferson's Declaration, alongside Lincoln's Gettysburg Address and King's "I Have a Dream" civic sermon, remains one of America's most treasured expressions of secularized sacred rhetoric. Jefferson, however, also wrote *Notes on the State of Virginia*. When *Notes* is considered in a sociopsychological context (the brutish language about people of African descent) I am compelled to make an effort to understand Jefferson's intellectual and emotional contradictions which point toward his double consciousness. This is significant because Jefferson's humanism, idealism, and religious views influenced the founding social conditions and philosophical points of departure that shaped and birthed the University of Virginia. It is his university, therefore, that I believe has a fiduciary duty, if not moral obligation, to redeem Mr. Jefferson's human contradictions by engaging in the ministry of reconciliation.

NOTES

1. Brent D. Glass, "Foreword," in Thomas Jefferson, *The Jefferson Bible: The Life and Morals of Jesus of Nazareth Extracted Textually from the Gospels in Greek, Latin, French, and English* (Washington, DC: Smithsonian, 2011), 6.

2. Kevin R. C. Gutzman, *Thomas Jefferson Revolutionary: A Radical's Struggle to Remake America* (New York: St. Martin's Press, 2017), 97.

3. Ibid., 99.

4. Harry R. Rubenstein and Barbara Clark Smith, "History of the Jefferson Bible," *The Jefferson Bible*, 25.

5. Ibid., 15.

6. John B. Boles, *Jefferson: Architect of American Liberty* (New York: Basic Books, 2017), 81.

7. Ibid., 80.

8. Rubenstein and Smith, *The Jefferson Bible*, 23. Jefferson was influenced by theologian Joseph Priestley's *An History of the Corruptions of Christianity*, written in England in 1782. Priestly held that science would demystify the world and ultimately undermine political and religious authorities who promoted superstition to maintain their "undue and usurped authority."

9. David Hume, *A Treatise of Human Nature*, ed. Ernest C. Mossner (New York: Penguin Classics, 1985), 7. The excerpt is a part of Mossner's introduction to Hume's classic.

10. Cornel West, *The Cornel West Reader* (New York: Basic Civitas Books, 1999), 83.

11. Ibid., 84.

12. Henry Louis Gates Jr., *The Signifying Monkey: A Theory of African American Literary Criticism* (Oxford: Oxford University Press, 2014), 73.

13. Thomas Jefferson, *Notes on the State of Virginia* (New York: Penguin Books, 1999), 147.

14. Rubenstein and Smith, *The Jefferson Bible*, 16–17.

15. David Hume, "Against Miracles," in *Philosophy of Religion: An Anthology*, eds. Louis P. Pojman and Michael Rea (Stamford, CT: Cengage Learning, 2015), 458.

16. Ibid., 461.

17. Rubenstein and Smith, *The Jefferson Bible*, 11.

18. Ibid., 17.

19. Ibid., 23.

20. Ibid., 17.

21. Ibid., 23.

22. Ibid.

23. Ibid., 25.

24. Brent D. Glass, *The Jefferson Bible*, 7.

25. Rubenstein and Smith, *The Jefferson Bible*, 30.

26. Jefferson, *Notes*, ix.

27. Susan Tyler Hitchcock, *The University of Virginia: A Pictorial History* (Charlottesville: University of Virginia Press, 2012), viii.

28. "UVa Names Dorm after Former Slaves," *News and Advance* (originally in *The* [Charlottesville] *Daily Progress*, July 15, 2015), http://www.newsadvance.com/uva-names-dorm-after-former-slaves/article_bb766c5d-2197-5660-991d-9dd9544054d0.html, accessed May 31, 2017.

29. See chapter 1.

30. See "How Diverse Is University of Virginia—Main Campus?", *College Factual*, http://www.collegefactual.com/colleges/university-of-virginia-main-campus/student-life/diversity, accessed May 17, 2017.

31. See "University of Virginia," *College Atlas*, https://www.collegeatlas.org/university-of-virginia.html, accessed May 31, 2017.

32. Ben Myers, "The Flagship Diversity Divide," *The Chronicle of Higher Education* (January 5, 2016), http://www.chronicle.com/interactives/flagship-diversity, accessed June 1, 2017.

33. Ibid.

34. Ibid.*The Chronicle* has calculated the Diversity Index for every state's flagship university. Myers points out that they have counted racial and ethnic diversity among students and full-time professors. In addition, there were comparisons of scores in specific ways, such as scores with state-level numbers. They used university data reported to the Department of Education for the 2013–2014 academic year and state census data for 2010.

35. University of Virginia, President's Commission on Slavery and the University, http://slavery.virginia.edu/, accessed June 1, 2017.

36. Ibid. See also Brown University Steering Committee on Slavery and Justice, http://www.brown.edu/Research/Slavery_Justice/; Emory University, Office of Equality and Inclusion, http://equityandinclusion.emory.edu/; University of North Carolina, the Louis Round Wilson Library, http://library.unc.edu/wilson, accessed June 1, 2017.

Afterword

Since the writing of *Reconciliation and Reparation: Preaching Economic Justice*, Rev. Dr. Wyatt Tee Walker has died (August 16, 1929—January 23, 2018). His death signifies that an era has passed and that a new prophetic leadership paradigm shift must emerge. Walker was one of the towering iconic figures in what is now a globalized human rights struggle. Walker's theological worldview evolved; he described his theology as informed by pan-Africanism.[1] Indeed he provided direct affirmation for my own emergent pan-African theological worldview and my pursuit for justice through economic reparations. Walker came to national and international prominence through the significant role that he had in the desegregation of the American South. He served as Dr. Martin Luther King Jr.'s chief of staff and as the Civil Rights Movement's principal strategist.

Without Walker, American civil rights campaigns would not have been successful and the historic March on Washington would not have occurred. All have seen the grainy black and white film footage of Dr. King's funeral processional. All have noticed the two mules that pulled the old caisson which carried Dr. King's casket draped with Old Glory. The processional was King's last organized liberation march, because Coretta Scott King entrusted the funeral plan and logistical details to Dr. Wyatt Tee Walker.[2] The Du Boisan–like Silent March was three miles in length, the distance between Ebenezer Baptist Church where King served as pastor and Morehouse College, King's alma mater. Indeed, perhaps this organized liberation march provided an answer to Tertullian's question, "What does Athens have to do with Jerusalem?"[3]

After the King era, Walker adapted to new and global realities. He understood that the struggle for civil rights had to evolve into forms of global interdependence among Asians and Africans—for all people of color to achieve global human rights. Over time, Walker's views changed over America's capacity to erase the stains of an unrelenting racist culture, a culture that has continued to pull racist levers of manipulation and exploitation over all socio-marginalized people groups, but which continued to be pointed primarily toward people of African descent in America. As civil rights leaders began to consider American commitment to eradication of the underprivileged and underemployment in the post-King era, one thing became clear to Walker: he did not see a national commitment to eradicating racism and poverty at home or internationally.

Walker came to this conclusion because the dominating culture's institutional spheres resisted the Poor People's Campaign, which was a planned mass movement and a strategic effort to reorient American politics and policies. However, the Vietnam War usurped President Lyndon Johnson's War on Poverty. Billions of dollars were spent to fund the conflict in Vietnam, dollars that Walker believed should have been used to redistribute income and wealth and to provide other human services.[4] (It should be noted here that Wyatt Tee Walker and James Bevell made numerous attempts to force Dr. King to publicly denounce the Vietnam War sooner; King did first speak publicly against the Vietnam War at a Southern Christian Leadership Conference (SCLC) regional meeting at Virginia State University in Petersburg, Virginia. The year was 1966.[5])

As a response to the changing political climate, an organized liberation protest, which had been planned for May 2, 1968 in Washington, DC, evolved into what is commonly referred to as Tent City. The organized liberation movement was to demand fairer distribution of wealth in America. Without this redistribution, there could not be major breakthroughs against racism.[6]

Without King's leadership presence, the Poor People's Campaign did not gain the sociopolitical and moral traction needed to make quantum policy leaps and economic advancements. One reason for this may have been that in the middle 1960s, King, along with Walker, found that the Du Boisian construct of race, economics, and politics continued to exist in Middle America (where churches appeared increasingly attracted to a fascist kind of religion similar to what had emerged in Nazi Germany in the 1930s), in the United States government apparatus (at federal, state, and local levels), and on Wall Street. Therefore, the mass demonstration campaign was necessary but not fully supported by key institutions with influence in economic, political, and religious domains.

A second reason for the Campaign's decline may have been King's own untimely death. His death created a deep wound in the psyche of people of color around the world. In the United States, the Movement's Kingless leadership lost political support from sympathetic federal lawmakers in Washington. Shortly after King's assassination, the United States government and other important partners aborted its fight against eradicating poverty and, yes, racism. Human rights would take a back seat to other pressing political concerns in America. There were no doubts left in anyone's mind: America had entered a post-King era, an era that would bring us the military and prison industrial complexes.

These point toward a third reason for the Campaign's faltering, namely that the nation had shifted toward a globalized capitalism—a full court press. Walker ceased to believe that universal human rights could be achieved through the leadership of the dominating imperial hegemonic state in the world—the United States. In the era of Trump, it is becoming clearer daily that America's jurisprudence, politics, and dominating culture's religion do not have the stomach to face that income and wealth inequalities are major factors in our declining trust in dominating culture's public and private institutions. In other words, America's public and private institutional spheres have stopped short of complete socio-integration. By socio-integration, I mean a universal effort that is accomplished by moving at all deliberate speed toward economic fairness that should be reinforced by policies which lead the nation and ultimately the global village closer to achieving income and wealth equalities. What has occurred is nothing more than desegregation by law. This is at the heart of this book's thesis: *Effective twenty-first-century preaching is prophetic when it addresses closing the income and wealth gap.*

Walker's theological worldview is similar to that of W. E. B. Du Bois. Du Boisian thinkers grasp the unrivaled significance of Du Bois's race, economics, and politics construct, something that Du Bois considered as a nearly inseparable part of the psyche of the dominating Western cultural pathology. It is a pathology that reinforces sociopolitical and permanent race castes; it reinforces market-driven imperial economies.[7] Walker was a Du Boisian thinker and deeply rooted in the Du Bosian prophetic tradition. It was the Du Boisian prophetic tradition that influenced Walker's reading and interpretation of the Old and New Testaments. He understood that the historical Jesus was a Palestinian Jew and a revolutionary leader[8] and that both Testaments are liberation documents, with liberation narratives. Moreover, Walker recognized and affirmed that both Testaments' liberation narratives have organized liberation marches toward human justice.

At the taproot of this book is an effort to craft an alternative narrative. The narrative informs a prophetic rhetoric and rhetorical theory which are necessary in order to confront and overcome human inequalities (the income and wealth gap). This is the assignment of the twenty-first-century black church, which I commonly refer to as the twenty-first-century's Church of People of African Descent. I call its preachers Du Boisian preachers, men and women committed to the biblical and Du Boisian prophetic traditions.

In short, we must grapple with what can only be described as our clear and present danger. This is a quasi-definition for an existential threat to humanity. What is more, I have placed the largest burden of responsibility into the hands of the twenty-first-century black church. It is my view that the Church of People of African Descent must recognize and address this existential threat. In order to exist—quite literally to exist—Du Boisian preachers must preach sermons that confront this threat directly and persuade the Church of People of African Descent that this proclamation of reconciliation and reparation is our major focus—or by definition our preaching is not prophetic.

Dr. Wyatt Tee Walker (among others) has provided a guidepost for us to follow. Dr. Walker inspired and mentored me; he read some of this book's early chapter drafts—and he chose me to preach his eulogy. Thus his spirit and his commitment charge us to pursue Jesus of Nazareth's kingdom of God in the human realm. This book serves as a challenge to its readers: we must rediscover our divine assignment and purpose. In this book, I have written that our assignment and purpose is to proclaim the radicalized gospel, given to us by the radicalized life ethic and words of Jesus of Nazareth that includes reconciliation and reparation. We must rediscover Walker-like courage to confront empire and its imperialistic cultures and economies. If we refuse this awestruck assignment, I believe that our country and world as we know it will continue to devolve into total dehumanization and will not be able to recover. Thus, we must prophetically preach reconciliation and reparation in the twenty-first century, and that begins within the pulpits of the black church.

Joseph Evans
Bennett Hall, 2018

NOTES

1. See Wyatt Tee Walker, *Afrocentrism and Christian Faith* (New York: Martin Luther King Fellows, 1993).

2. Wyatt Tee Walker, *The King of Love: My Days with Martin Luther King Jr.*, unpublished manuscript, 7. This is from Dr. Walker's unfinished draft, which he presented to me in 2017.

3. See James McGrath, blog post, http://www.patheos.com/blogs/religion-prof/2008/02/what-has-athens-to-do-with-jerusalem.html. Accessed February 24, 2018.

4. Martin Luther King Jr., "Where Do We Go from Here?" in *A Testament of Hope: The Essential Writings and Speeches of Martin Luther King Jr.* (HarperCollins, 1991), 248. King said, "Now our country can do this [eradicate poverty]. John Kenneth Galbraith said that a guaranteed annual income could be done for about twenty billion dollars a year. And I say to you today, that if our nation can spend thirty-five billion dollars to fight an unjust war, [an] evil war in Vietnam, and twenty billion dollars to put a man on the moon, it can spend billions of dollars to put God's children on their feet right here on earth."

5. See *A Testament of Hope*, 55.

6. Walker, *The King of Love*, 28.

7. W. E. B. Du Bois, *Dusk of Dawn: An Essay toward an Autobiography of a Race Concept* (Piscataway, NJ: Transaction Publishers, 2011). In the book's Introduction, Irene Diggs wrote, "It was after Du Bois left Harvard, while at the University of Berlin, that he began to envision the race problem in the United States to include the problems of the peoples of Africa, Asia, the economics and politics of Europe. He began to see 'clearly the connection of economics and politics; the fundamental influence of man's efforts to earn a living upon all his other efforts.' He realized how the building of colonial empires 'turned into the threat of armed competition for markets, cheap material and cheap labor.' For him, economics and politics were inextricably

intertwined; he perceived politics as dominant, but because most Blacks were workers and earners of wages he was fascinated by economics" (ix–x). Du Bois himself wrote, "I began to see the race problem in America, the problem of the peoples of Africa and Asia, and the political development of Europe as one. I began to unite my economics and politics; but I still assumed that in these groups of activities and forces, the political realm was dominant" (47).

8. Wyatt Tee Walker, "Liberation Theology and the Conflict in the Middle East" in *A Prophet from Harlem Speaks: Sermons and Essays* (New York: Martin Luther King Fellows Press, 1998), 73–74.